Fundamentals of Cultural Psychology

This innovative textbook is the ideal introduction to cultural psychology. It focuses on a holistic approach, which emphasizes that culture is created and shared by minds and society.

Organized around short core concept chapters, the book encourages students to think critically about culture and the theories around it. Chapters explore what cultural psychology is and its forms of knowing, how cultural psychology can be used to understand higher psychological functions, and the human psyche as a whole. Each chapter contains definitions of key concepts, real-world examples from everyday human activities, reflection questions, short biographies of key figures relevant to cultural psychology, and chapter summaries. There are also links to video interviews from leading international scholars, which provide critical reflections on core concepts in cultural psychology.

This is the essential introductory book for students of cultural psychology, as well as cultural studies and anthropology. It will be useful for anyone looking to learn more about the history of ideas, the human mind, and its historical and material relationship with culture.

Luca Tateo is Professor in Epistemology, Theory, and Methodology of Qualitative Research at the University of Oslo, Norway, and Visiting Associate Professor at the Federal University of Bahia, Brazil. He is co-editor in chief of the journal *Human Arenas: An Interdisciplinary Journal of Psychology, Culture, and Meaning*.

'Luca Tateo's *Fundamentals of Cultural Psychology* is a rare achievement: It is both student-friendly and inviting at the same time that it is an intellectually challenging contribution to this rapidly growing field of study.'

– **Michael Cole**, *Emeritus Distinguished Professor at the University of California, San Diego (UCSD)*

'This text book about the fundamentals of cultural psychology is bound to be a classic. Professor Luca Tateo offers a new, clear, and compelling vision of cultural psychology that transcends disciplinary boundaries and geographies. The story of cultural psychology narrated here is drawn from philosophy, history, medicine, sociology, anthropology, art, and humanities, and theology. This textbook achieves a rare feat of creating a truly mind-opening learning experience for beginning and advanced students of psychology. This book offers a valuable resource for anyone who is genuinely interested in deepening their inquiry and transforming their understanding of the field of cultural psychology.'

– **Sunil Bhatia**, *Lucy Marsh Haskell '19 Professor of Human Development at Connecticut College*

Fundamentals of Cultural Psychology

LUCA TATEO

LONDON AND NEW YORK

Cover image: Paul Rhodes

First published 2025
by Routledge
4 Park Square, Milton Park, Abingdon, Oxon OX14 4RN

and by Routledge
605 Third Avenue, New York, NY 10158

Routledge is an imprint of the Taylor & Francis Group, an informa business

© 2025 Luca Tateo

The right of Luca Tateo to be identified as author of this work has been asserted in accordance with sections 77 and 78 of the Copyright, Designs and Patents Act 1988.

All rights reserved. No part of this book may be reprinted or reproduced or utilised in any form or by any electronic, mechanical, or other means, now known or hereafter invented, including photocopying and recording, or in any information storage or retrieval system, without permission in writing from the publishers.

Trademark notice: Product or corporate names may be trademarks or registered trademarks, and are used only for identification and explanation without intent to infringe.

British Library Cataloguing-in-Publication Data
A catalogue record for this book is available from the British Library

Library of Congress Cataloging-in-Publication Data
Names: Tateo, Luca, author.
Title: Fundamentals of cultural psychology / Luca Tateo.
Description: New York : Routledge, 2024. | Includes bibliographical references and index.
Identifiers: LCCN 2024015093 (print) | LCCN 2024015094 (ebook) | ISBN 9781138576841 (hbk) | ISBN 9781138576872 (pbk) | ISBN 9781351268721 (ebk)
Subjects: LCSH: Ethnopsychology—Textbooks.
Classification: LCC GN502 .T38 2024 (print) | LCC GN502 (ebook) | DDC 155.8/2—dc23/eng/20240703
LC record available at https://lccn.loc.gov/2024015093
LC ebook record available at https://lccn.loc.gov/2024015094

ISBN: 9781138576841 (hbk)
ISBN: 9781138576872 (pbk)
ISBN: 9781351268721 (ebk)

DOI: 10.4324/9781351268721

Typeset in Times New Roman
by Apex CoVantage, LLC

Access the Support Material: routledge.com/9781138576872

Contents

    Foreword   ix

Introduction   1
The perspective of the book 2
Structure of the volume 3
How to use this book 5
References 6

1   **Basic concepts**   7
    Chapter overview 9
    Group activity for instructor: cogenetic logic 9
    Beyond binaries: the cogenetic logic 10
    Concepts as systems in cultural psychology 12
    The human being as meaning-maker 15
    Surplus of meaning 18
    Group activity for instructor: different types of signs 20
    Signs and semiosis 20
    Signs and meaning-making 24
    Mediation 25
    Activity and artifact 27
    From the world to the psyche and back: the internalization/
        externalization cycle 30
    Summary of Chapter 1 33

2   **The forms of knowing**   37
    Chapter overview 38
    Group activity for the instructor: the letter 38

Temporality 39
Irreversible time 39
Time as context 42
Dialogicality 44
Narrativity 46
Qualitative methods to study developing living systems 53
Summary of Chapter 2 56

3 What is cultural psychology? 59

Chapter overview 60
Group activity for instructor: what is your culture? 60
Culture as cultivation: the Norwegian house 60
Do we need culture? 63
First, second, and third nature 67
Cultural psychology 69
A bit of history 70
Collective culture and personal culture 72
Window of acceptable possibilities 73
In-between cultures 76
Decolonizing the study of cultures 78
An ecological approach to mind and culture 79
The zone of potential estrangement 80
Summary of Chapter 3 82

4 Imagination 87

Chapter overview 88
Group activities for instructor 88
Do we know or do we imagine? 89
Knowing by imagining 91
Imagination as uncoupling 93
Imagining future worlds: mental experiments and utopias 94
Expansive and reductive imagination 97
The theory of imaginative process as a higher mental function 98
The sociogenesis of imagining 100
Educating imagining 102
Imagining as a higher mental function 103
Summary of Chapter 4 105

5 Borders 109

Chapter overview 110
Group activity for instructor: borders 110
Borders and bordering in the environment and in the mind 110
Cultural psychology of borders 113
Borders and mind 113
Borders and signs 115

The developmental function of borders: the concept of *Gegenstand* 116
Selective internalization of borders 119
The general genetic law of bordering development 121
Summary of Chapter 5 124

6   **The psyche as dynamic totality**   **127**

Chapter overview 128
Group activity for instructor: affectivating 128
Are human beings coherent? 129
Dilemmas 130
Ambivalence 134
The semiotics of ambivalence 138
Tensegrity 142
Affective logic 147
Summary of Chapter 6 152

Index 155

Foreword

THE GLORY AND MISERY OF TEXTBOOKS

It is my great pleasure to write this Foreword to the new book by Luca Tateo with whom we have worked for two decades. He is a person of great determination – the goal of creating this first real textbook of cultural psychology required much patience, creativity, and – above all – imagination. There were no good models for textbooks in psychology ahead of him, in any area of psychology. He invented a new one – with the focus on promoting students' constructive imagination. This is particularly evident in the quiet humor of the illustrations. It is a textbook that opens readers' minds to new ideas, rather than defines the scope of orthodoxy of the given field of knowledge.

Why is the *textbook* genre inherently ambivalent? Its role – bearing in mind the need of learners to gain access to the basic knowledge in the given field – should present that basic knowledge of a given science as it is. Yet no corpus of knowledge is ever fixed as it is – all science grows from what is considered basic. Thus scientific knowledge is never finite – yet textbooks present it *as if it is*. Michael Polanyi expressed that paradox succinctly:

> Scientific discovery reveals new knowledge, but the new vision that accompanies it is not knowledge. It is *less* than knowledge, for it is a guess; but it is *more* than knowledge, for it is a foreknowledge of things unknown and at present perhaps inconceivable. Our vision of the general nature of things is our guide for the interpretation of all future experience. Such guidance is indispensable. Theories of the scientific method which try to explain the establishment of scientific truth by any purely objective formal procedure are doomed to failure. Any process of enquiry unguided by intellectual passions would inevitably spread out into a desert of trivialities.
>
> (Polanyi, 1962, p. 135)

Cultural psychology is one of the recent inventions in psychology for which becoming an orthodox framework of fixed knowledge would be epistemologically suicidal. Integrating knowledge from art, history, biology, and semiotics into psychology, cultural psychology leads the way out of the many crises that psychology has been in – its search for itself as a science. Teaching in a new field requires demand for creativity by the learners. This guidance for openness to innovation is the key feature of this textbook. It gently guides the readers – who are eager to learn how to transcend the knowhow of the teachers – to create new knowledge. This is the special artful mastery of Luca Tateo – the liberation of learning minds from the avalanche of brief trivialities of unreflective messages that have become standard in social media practices of the 21st century and that enslave human imagination.

Jaan Valsiner
Aalborg and Salvador (Bahia), February 2024

REFERENCE

Polanyi, M. (1962). *Personal knowledge*. London: Routledge & Kegan Paul.

Introduction

Almost fourteen years have passed between the first insight into this book and its publication. In between, a whole nomadic trajectory of research questions, challenges, insights, travels, encounters, and reflections. I first came into contact with cultural psychology as a doctoral student who was totally dissatisfied and impatient with psychology as it was socialized in the academic context. At that time, I had the opportunity to meet Jaan Valsiner, who later became my mentor and friend, during a summer school. Later, I understood that the serendipity of that encounter was quite common among people who feel somehow out of place in the current academic culture. Cultural psychology appeared to me as a mind-opening experience, and a means to explore new territories in the way human beings think, feel, create, destroy, and relate to each other and to their environment. I was certainly predisposed to this meeting, being educated at the University of Salerno in the intellectual tradition of Pina Boggi Cavallo, whose humanistic background and deep commitment to the complexities of human experience resisted the technocratic drift of much of contemporary psychology (Marsico & Tateo, 2023).

Thanks to the encounter with cultural psychology, I was granted access to a global interdisciplinary community – woven from the countless travels of Jaan Valsiner and coagulated around that wonderful place of free intellectual exchange which is the Kitchen Seminar – in which I had the opportunity to meet so many great and innovative scholars: Pina Marsico, thanks to whom I developed most of my past and current ideas, Robert Innis, Nandita Chaudhary, Virginia Dazzani, Raffaele De Luca Picione, Livia Simão and Danilo Guimarães, Shuangshuang Xu, Kevin Carriere, and Lado

Gamsakhurdia. I am just dropping a few names among the hundreds of students, those just starting their careers, and the senior colleagues I met on this journey – and with whom I collaborated in an infinite number of research and editorial projects. I have been so lucky to be part of a global intellectual circle of people who are intolerant of academic hierarchies and power structures, deeply passionate with their research questions, and open to otherness. As a student, I had the opportunity to meet people who were interested in my ideas rather than my age or status and I have tried to disseminate the same model in my academic work.

The idea of this textbook slowly emerged with the awareness that the most commonly available academic instruction volumes, especially in the Global North, were progressively becoming poorer in their presentation of the history of psychological ideas and the diversity of approaches, not acknowledging the dialogue with other forms of knowledge, and dogmatic in reducing psychology to a specific tradition of study (Valsiner, 2017). If one looks at the main figures of the history of psychology – from its origins in the 17th to 18th centuries to the first half of the 20th century – it is easy to see how the background of the main thinkers and innovators was diverse and articulated. Doing psychology required one to be learned also in philosophy, history, medicine, sociology, anthropology, art and humanities, and even theology – all interdisciplinary competences (or rather, humanistic education) that are no longer offered to students nowadays. Cultural psychology is a crossroads and interdisciplinary field because it is interested in the variety of human activities and sometimes its texts are quite complex and require a lot of additional knowledge. So, the necessity of an introductory textbook began to become clear. I started to collect the results of my teaching practice and that of my colleagues, to design specific teaching activities to introduce students to unfamiliar concepts, and all these materials, together with the scientific literature, have now come together in this book.

THE PERSPECTIVE OF THE BOOK

Cultural psychology is the study of third-level psychological processes, such as meaning-making, imagining, constructive remembering, affectivating; bordering, and teaching/learning. Third-level psychological processes are those complex personal and collectively coordinated human experiences that presuppose the hierarchical dynamic integration of lower level (perception, attention, etc.) and higher-level mental functions (language, memory, reflection, etc.). Third-level psychological processes cannot be reduced to lower levels nor can they be considered in terms of single separated functions. They constitute a systemic organization, in which whole–parts hierarchical integration makes the process possible. It follows that the object of interest of cultural psychology is not a single psychic function or a single sub-module of neural activity. As a matter of fact, cultural psychology is not even one among the specialized branches of psychological sciences. I would rather say that it is a way to look at human psychic phenomena so that one can find a cultural psychology of education, a cultural psychology of work, a cultural psychology of gender, a cultural psychology of development, etc.

Of course, the perspective about cultural psychology that I provide in this textbook is partial, as any perspective. It is mainly based on the contributions I acquired from Valsiner's semiotic approach, the cultural–historical theory, the Tartu school of ecosemiotics, the decolonizing and feminist perspective, and my personal background in Mediterranean humanities. Pretending to be impartial is indeed a sign of dogmatism. Partiality also implies that you need a counterpart, a complementary perspective, an antithesis, a dance partner, to develop any type of reasoning.

STRUCTURE OF THE VOLUME

This textbook is meant to be used in an introductory course in cultural psychology at BA or MA level of 6–8 weeks' duration. Of course, it is also a good textbook for all the curricula in psychology, cultural studies, anthropology, history of ideas, and humanities in general that provide students with knowledge about the human mind in its historical and material relationships with culture.

Each chapter of the book covers one of the basic areas of interest for the student who is approaching cultural psychology for the first time. Chapter 1, "Basic concepts", introduces the fundamental concepts of cultural psychology, their definitions, and how they can be located in different arenas of human activity. These concepts represent the bricks that the instructor and the student can use to construct the conceptual building blocks of cultural psychology. Cultural psychology is highly interdisciplinary and theory-driven, so many of the concepts are also used in other social and human sciences. The concepts of cogenetic logic, sign, semiosis, meaning-making, activity, mediation, artifact, and the internalization/externalization cycle are the axiomatic principles on which is based an understanding of the human psyche in cultural psychology.

Chapter 2, "The forms of knowing", introduces the methodology of cultural psychology. We describe the epistemological principles and explain what types of knowledge and what types of research questions can be created in cultural psychology. Then, we discuss the methodological principles, that is the types of strategies and instruments we can construct to answer the research questions and to produce knowledge. The research questions of cultural psychology always focus on the genesis and development of human psychological phenomena, which unfold in time and space, in relation to others but in a unique personal form. The epistemological principles we present are the concepts of temporality, dialogicality, and narrativity and how they shape our common knowledge. The methodology in cultural psychology is instead always qualitative, in the sense that it is interested in the unique qualities of psychological experience, regardless of the mix of techniques that can be used. In contrast to other types of psychological science, cultural psychology is not interested in the inductive accumulation of empirical evidence. We are instead looking for the significant specimen of the phenomena that can be theoretically generalized. In other words, we are not studying any "average" assemblage of variables but are interested in defining theoretically significant profiles of unique cases.

Chapter 3, "What is cultural psychology", is the moment in which we dare to provide a definition of cultural psychology, which is not another academic discipline but a peculiar way of understanding culture and its relationship with the mind. First, the chapter outlines the history of cultural psychology from the, of course, partial perspective of the semiotic approach (Valsiner, 2014). Then, we introduce the concept of personal culture and the concept of a window of acceptable possibilities. Afterwards, we discuss what happens between cultures and illustrate the concept of proculturation to understand what happens during a cultural transition. Finally, we discuss the difference between cultural psychology and cross-cultural psychology; and the decolonization of psychology.

In Chapter 4, "Imagination", we show how cultural psychology can be used to understand higher psychological functions and, in particular, imagination. Then, we present the two main theories of imagination in cultural psychology and how imagination works in everyday life and in sociogenetic development. In Chapter 5, "Borders", we discuss the bordering process and the concept of borders and border crossing that have gained increasing importance for cultural psychology. The construction, crossing, and demolition of borders is a fundamental way of organizing both psychic experience and the environment. The border is a constitutive part of the triadic fundamental unit of analysis in cogenetic logic. We discuss the phenomenology of borders, their semiotic functioning, and the consequences of human psychological experience. Finally, we discuss the role of bordering in sociogenesis and present the general genetic law of bordering development and its role in psychological functioning.

Chapter 6, "The psyche as dynamic totality", closes the circle by outlining the idea of human psyche that emerges from the perspective of cultural psychology through its epistemological premises, its concepts, and its methodology. The psyche is understood as a dynamic totality based on affective logic and organized on the principle of tensegrity. The idea of dynamic totality is dialectically opposed to the classical idea of psychological processes as closure-seeking and dissonance-avoiding. The chapter describes the human experience in terms of non-linear processes that imply ambivalence, tension, and a dilemmatic field. The dynamic tension between continuity and discontinuity is fundamental to providing psychological functioning and development.

INTRODUCTION

HOW TO USE THIS BOOK

The book is constructed as an "open work" (Eco, 1989). Although we had in mind a certain ideal reader, the activities and the chapters are built in such a way that instructors and students can collaborate in customizing and expanding them.

The six chapters are imagined as topics for 1–2 weeks of work. The structure is the same for all of them. The chapter opens with a brief overview of the learning goals and then presents a class activity related to the chapter's topics. The activity is a suggestion that can be elaborated by the instructor and the students together. I warmly invite the instructors to imagine new activities.

Each chapter contains some concepts, their definitions, some examples from everyday human activities, and the contextualization of the concepts in the history of ideas. You will also find some additional content such as boxes with short biographies of historical figures whose ideas are relevant for cultural psychology. Those boxes are meant to invite students to read more about those people that are sometimes forgotten in mainstream texts. The knowledge of the history of psychology is often overlooked in current curricula but it is essential to understand the genesis of ideas and to avoid reinventing the wheel (Valsiner, 2017). Besides, direct access to the thinking of past scholars can be very helpful to identify fruitful ideas that have not been fully developed and can still contribute to knowledge development.

Each chapter ends with a summary of the main concepts and with a collaborative exercise of self-assessment and reflection. Students are required to take their time and think about what they learn, how this knowledge fits (or conflicts) with their previous ideas, and how they can use it to produce new insights. The final task of each chapter is neither meant for academic assessment nor can be solved using artificial intelligence. The task is rather an invitation to use one's "organic" intelligence, critical thinking, educated intuition, and personal commitment to understand how human psyche functions in relation to culture.

Finally, there is an interesting additional feature. On some pages, you will find a QR-code that can be scanned and used to access additional online content. If you follow the link, you will land on the book website and you will find some videoclips in which leading international scholars will provide brief definitions and critical reflections about some of the core concepts (e.g., culture, sign, artifact, etc.).

My wish is that students will find the textbook interesting and will be lured into more readings, accepting the inclusion of the cultural psychology perspective in their own research interests. I also hope that this book is the starting point of a growing body of knowledge and practices fertilized by the experiences of instructors and students worldwide. More than ever, we need scholars who care about the important existential questions of the present and the future: how to eliminate injustice and violence; how to live in harmony as part of a planetary ecosystem; how to make art flourish rather than war; how to help people meaningfully enjoy their lives. The most important textbook of cultural psychology is still to be written, and the authors will be those with passion and curiosity.

REFERENCES

Eco, U. (1989). *The open work*. Cambridge, MA: Harvard University Press.
Marsico, G., & Tateo, L. (Eds.) (2023). *Humanity in psychology: The intellectual legacy of Pina Boggi Cavallo*. Cham: Springer.
Valsiner, J. (2014). *An invitation to cultural psychology*. London: Sage.
Valsiner, J. (2017). *A guided science: History of psychology in the mirror of its making*. London: Routledge.

CHAPTER 1

Basic concepts

Scan the QR-code to access additional materials and watch outstanding international scholars discussing key concepts.

> **LEARNING GOALS**
>
> 1. To acquire the basic concepts of cultural psychology
> 2. To understand the way cultural psychology conceptualizes human meaning-making
> 3. To understand the epistemological principles of cultural psychology

Basic concepts

CHAPTER OVERVIEW

In this chapter, we present the fundamental concepts of cultural psychology, their definitions, and use. These concepts represent the basic bricks that we will use to construct the conceptual building of cultural psychology. Although they are used in other social and human sciences, concepts such as cogenetic logic, sign, semiosis, meaning-making, activity, mediation, artifact, and the internalization/externalization cycle are the axiomatic principles on which the understanding of human psyche is based.

GROUP ACTIVITY FOR INSTRUCTOR: COGENETIC LOGIC

Set up a whiteboard or an empty Power Point slide. Start by asking students: "How many objects do you see here?" pointing at the blank page. Collect student answers, and always remember to ask "Why?" to each of them. After a first round of responses, draw a circle in the middle of the page and ask: "And now, how many objects do you see here?". Students will start changing their answers. They will answer "One", "Two". Remember to always inquire "Why?" if they do not give an explanation spontaneously. After the second round, delete the circle and ask again, "And now, how many objects do you see here?". At the third round of questioning, you can start asking the students: "What action did I perform? How did it change the number of objects?".

BASIC CONCEPTS

Reflection questions
The activity is aimed at facilitating the understanding of cogenetic logic's principle: every act of distinction-making immediately produces a triadic system. To transfer the idea to different domains, reflect on the following questions:

1. Can I think about other examples of borders that create sets of three elements such as the inside-circle-outside in Figure 1.1?
2. Who draws the border and how in different social situations?
3. Can the border be changed, how, and by whom?

BEYOND BINARIES: THE COGENETIC LOGIC

If anyone asks: "What is the opposite of male?", "What is the opposite of rich?", or "What is the opposite of nature?", you will probably answer "female", "poor", or "culture" respectively, without much hesitation. This is indeed how people think and organize the categories that describe the world in common sense, but often also in social sciences. One seldom finds a study in which "male" and "female" are not included as independent variables, assuming their theoretical relevance. Sometimes the researchers can introduce a third option such as "other" or "none of the above", but the principle of having mutually exclusive categories is still present. In other words, social sciences like to create binary categories to classify phenomena. It seems natural and logical to classify the world into discrete and mutually exclusive categories. After all, we have known, since Aristotle, that things and people have an "identity" that cannot be confused with other "identities". "A" is equal to "A" and is not equal to "B" (in logic notation "A=A" and "A≠B" respectively). So, we tend to learn concepts in pairs as if they were opposites. For instance, we learn that a forest is part of "nature", and its opposite, such as a building, may be made by human "culture". In the same vein, we learn that a member of our national community is a "citizen", while those who do not belong to the same community are "foreigners". It sounds so natural that we end up believing that the pairs of opposites we learn in everyday life exist in reality (Tateo, 2020). However, in strictly logical terms, the opposite of concept "A" is its negation "non-A". Thus, the logic opposites, for example, of "male", "white", or "rich" should be "non-male", "non-white", and "non-rich", respectively. How does our perspective change if we try to form pairs of concepts in this way?

Reflection question: can you think about what is "non-rich", "non-male". or "non-white", etc? Who would you include in those categories, and why?

The sociologist P. G. Herbst (2012) tried to develop a new logic to understand the way human beings experience "the relation between our intentions and the conceptual and rational forms in terms of which we perceive and respond to ourselves and the environment" (Herbst, 2012, p. 84). He assumed that the primary operation necessary to organize experience – the genetic basis of logic and behavior – is the production of a *distinction* in

BASIC CONCEPTS

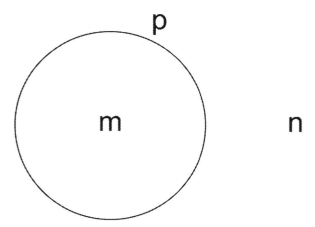

Figure 1.1 Herbst's triadic set

the undistinguished field or flow of events. As in the group activity at the beginning of the chapter, Herbst assumed that the single primary operation of creating a boundary can actualize a triadic set of elements (m, n, p; Figure 1.1).

The first axiom of his behavioral logic reads: "The primary conceptual unit is given as a triad of distinguishable undefined components, which are definable in terms of one another" (Herbst, 2012, p. 90). In a previously undistinguished original state, none of the elements was present. Once we draw the circumference "p", immediately we obtain an element "m", which is internal to the distinction, and an element "n" which is external. Again, with "the removal of the boundary, a distinction between inside and outside is no longer possible. The same result is obtained if either the inside or the outside is eliminated, for then also the other two components of the triad disappear as well" (Herbst, 2012, p. 89). Herbst proposed different examples of triads: (a) inside, outside, boundary; (b) finite region, infinite region, boundary; and (c) being, non-being, boundary (Figure 1.2). Those examples show how removing one of the elements of the triad makes the other disappear or become indistinguishable.

This type of logic is also called *cogenetic* (Tateo, 2016) because all the parts of the triad appear, are mutually defined, and disappear together as a whole. Thus, when one produces a conceptual distinction, for example by defining a category of "male", one immediately implies the existence of its logic complementary negation "non-male" and of a border that defines what is included in the set and what is included in the non-set. Now, try to imagine the consequences of redefining most of the concepts used in social sciences – which are formulated as dyadic structures (binaries) such as individualistic/collectivistic, qualitative/quantitative, marginal/mainstream, indigenous/universal, positive/negative, nature/nurture, stimulus/response, etc. – in the form of triadic structures of cogenetic logic.

Definition: the basic operation of cogenetic logic is the production of a distinction. It immediately produces a triadic system "A" –border – "non-A".

11

BASIC CONCEPTS

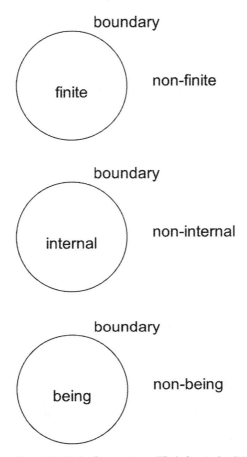

Figure 1.2 Triads of concepts, modified after Herbst (2012, p. 88)

CONCEPTS AS SYSTEMS IN CULTURAL PSYCHOLOGY

Cultural psychology overcomes false binaries and constructs its concepts as systems according to the *method of complementary negation* (Tateo, 2016). For every concept we use, we must be able to account for the whole composed by the triadic set (m, n, p; "A"+"non-A"+"distinction"). The guiding axiom of the cogenetic approach is that the triadic set always emerges as a whole, and none of the elements of the set can be deleted without making the whole disappear (Herbst, 2012). This implies the postulate that each element is codefined by the others. Even a concept that is apparently rooted in everyday experience, such as gender distinctions, is subject to this way of definition.

When defining the category of "masculine", for instance, one immediately evokes the complementary category of "non-masculine" and the way they are

BASIC CONCEPTS

Figure 1.3 Little sister and brother

distinguished. One assumes that this is something based on a given reality, as it is somehow closer to some representation of biology. If one considers the triadic system, instead, one realizes that throughout human history what is "masculine" and what is "non-masculine" (but not necessarily "feminine") have been subject to changes in meaning and mutual definitions (Figure 1.3).

In the portrait of the two young siblings, what could be considered in some contemporary cultures masculine and non-masculine attributes have a different relationship and meaning. Until the early 20th century, it was common practices to dress young boys, especially those belonging to affluent social classes, in dresses that would be considered "non-masculine" yet not "feminine". It is a clear example of how the triadic system of cogenetic logic allows more fine-grained understanding of human phenomena and their development over time.

What was previously included in the category of non-A can become, after a more or less long period of time, included in the category of A (for instance through assimilation, integration, etc.). The relationship A<>non-A (e.g. normal<>non-normal, moral<>non-moral, national<>non-national, inside<>non-inside, decent<>non-decent, etc.) is not an oppositional but a complementary one, an *inclusive separation* (Valsiner, 2014) in which

BASIC CONCEPTS

Reflection: if one cannot co-define the complementary "non-A" part of the cogenetic system, the concept is probably useless. For instance, to define the concept of "culture", one must also define the boundary of what is "non-culture". Otherwise, everything is "culture" and the all-encompassing concept becomes theoretically useless.

A<>non-A dynamically co-define each other, including a more or less large temporal and symbolic buffer zone (Figure 1.4) that establishes at the same time the rules of separation and the rules of permeability for the borders between A and non-A (Kullasepp & Marsico, 2021).

The bounded region (A), though remaining a closed set, can dynamically expand or constrict over time in the relationship with the open set (non-A) in the buffer region corresponding to the marginal instances of the person's integrity. This makes very interesting for cultural psychology all those forms of hybridization and marginality that dwell in buffer zones, and whose symbolic and material status can develop over time. For instance, all the different categories of immigrants, refugees, and nomads, or the spectrum of gender identities which are dynamically set as A<>non-A in the different conditions over time, probably always dwelling in the buffer zone, but changing as soon as the bounded region is expanded or constricted (dotted circles in Figure 1.4).

As we have seen, describing a concept (e.g. morality, culture, intelligence, etc.) implies the construction of a triadic system of meaning in which we are able to define (a) the operation of primary distinction (operator of segmentation or operator of displacement); (b) the closed set A; and (c) the complementary open set non-A. From the epistemological point of view, the common practice of establishing a conventional binary relationship of opposition between to concepts to understand them is a logical mistake.

A false logical negation created by opposing different concepts is in fact preventing any possibility of understanding and developing of one concept through the other (Figure 1.5). It is through the tension established between the elements (Valsiner, 2014) that the development of new meaning is made possible. As we have seen above, if one tries to define a concept like "masculine" by opposition with "feminine", one enters a binary and static system, failing to grasp the dynamics of the field of meanings. Instead, the method

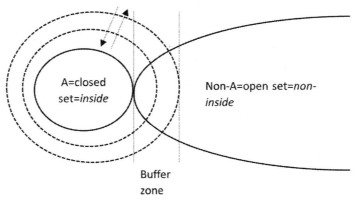

Figure 1.4 Dynamics of complementary sets

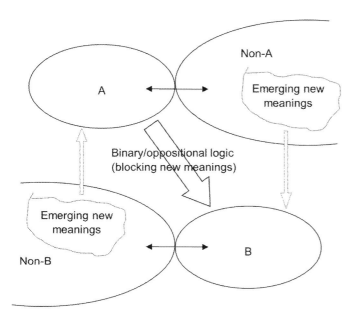

Figure 1.5 Cogenetic logic vs. oppositional logic

of complementary negation helps to define "masculine" through the complementary open set of "non-masculine" – which of course includes feminine, quasi-masculine, something not yet or no longer masculine, and so on – and must specify the conditions under which the distinction emerges and develops (who has the power of producing, maintaining, changing, and dismissing the distinction).

Such a non-dualistic epistemological framework has of course much in common with other non-dualistic perspectives, such as dialectics and Buddhism. However, the cogenetic logic introduces a triadic system in which the border or distinction plays a relevant role (see Chapter 5). Distinction-making is a primary act of organizing human experience, yet it does not produce a dualistic structure, which would not allow development (Figure 1.5). It creates a triadic system entailed with dynamic and tension (see Chapter 6) that accounts for developmental processes.

THE HUMAN BEING AS MEANING-MAKER

Human beings are compulsive meaning-makers (Valsiner, 2014). Every encounter with the world – whether the outer or the inner world – demands an attribution of meaning. If something is felt as "meaningless", it produces a sense of discomfort, frustration, and anguish that requires reparation (Frankl, 2010). The question "why" human beings make meaning of their lived experience is a question for philosophers or theologians. The "how" meanings are

BASIC CONCEPTS

produced, maintained, enacted, and demolished during psychological processes within collective life is the interest of cultural psychology.

> The history of the human species is that of breaking out from the dominance of the environment (adaptation to it) into a condition of future-oriented reflexivity – human beings adapt the environment not only to their current needs, but also to their anticipated, desired, and (often) unrealistic objectives (adaptation of the environment).
>
> (Valsiner, 2014, p. 148)

Meaning-making is (possibly) a human peculiarity that enabled human beings to shift from the mere reaction to environmental and endogenous stimuli (hunger, thirst, darkness, sudden noises, etc.) to more complex ways of interacting with the world and themselves. Imagine yourself before a corner (Figure 1.6). You may have different options: looking behind the corner, avoiding passing by the corner; just ignoring it; etc. However, any decision would entail a moment in which you would ask yourself "what's around the corner". If you are a professional writer, this would probably be the beginning of a novel. If you are walking in a street at night, this may be an anxiety-provoking experience. If you are a robber, this may be a potential opportunity.

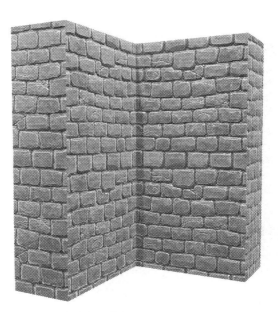

Figure 1.6 What's around the corner?

16

In all these cases, one would not merely respond to the shape and light of the corner. One would be compelled to start wondering what may be around the corner, making sense of it.

Classical psychology would describe it as *a need for cognitive closure* (Webster & Kruglanski, 1994), that is, the basic need of overcoming the ambiguity of stimuli to find a calm, consistent, and stable resolution. The idea of human inability to stand ambiguity and ambivalence for long has often been considered an axiom of psychological functioning (see Chapter 6). Yet, we know from personal experience that closure is *boring*. Most of mankind's greatest artistic production is such because it is not providing a *closure* pedantically. In his famous conversations with François Truffaut about cinema, Alfred Hitchcock illuminates the relationship between closure and tension:

> There is a distinct difference between 'suspense' and 'surprise,' [. . .] I'll explain what I mean. We are now having a very innocent little chat. Let's suppose that there is a bomb underneath this table between us. Nothing happens, and then all of a sudden, 'Boom!' There is an explosion. The public is surprised, but prior to this surprise, it has seen an absolutely ordinary scene, of no special consequence. Now, let us take a suspense situation. The bomb is underneath the table and the public knows it, probably because they have seen the anarchists place it there. The public is aware the bomb is going to explode at one o'clock and there is a clock in the decor. The public can see that it is a quarter to one. In such conditions, the same innocuous conversation becomes fascinating because the public is participating in the scene. [. . .] In the second we have provided them with fifteen minutes of suspense. The conclusion is that whenever possible the public must be informed. Except when the surprise is a twist, that is, when the unexpected ending is, in itself, the highlight of the story.
>
> (Truffaut & Hitchcock, 1985, p. 73)

As Hitchcock explains, the amount of information provided is not crucial in determining the experience of the audience. What matters is the fact that people (both authors and audiences) produce meaning in conditions of uncertainty, not necessarily to reduce uncertainty, rather to be in control of it, sometimes experiencing pleasure in enduring it or making it last. Meaning-making is constantly oriented towards "what's next", even when making sense of the past (see Chapter 4). Pedantic and pedagogic reduction of uncertainty is indeed a characteristic of authoritarian propaganda to reduce the range of potentially alternative and antagonistic interpretations, because it does not absolutely want people to produce meanings autonomously.

SURPLUS OF MEANING

Meaning-making is thus something that goes beyond the mere representation of, mirroring, or reaction to a stimulus. It is a process that produces something *more*. Humans tend to see things and fellow people *as something* under *certain conditions*. Sometimes the border between different categories of objects can be blurred. Sometimes it is not easy to decide whether something is alive or not; sometimes we treat pets like human beings (Figure 1.7) or we treat human beings as dehumanized objects (Figure 1.8).

Figure 1.7 Birthday celebrations for the White House family dog, 2009 (official White House photo by Pete Souza, retrieved from https://commons.wikimedia.org/wiki/File:P100909PS-0538_(4014569128).jpg)

Figure 1.8 Dehumanization leads to abject meaning-making: The Dinner in Brazil, by Jean-Baptiste Debret, 1839 lithograph (https://commons.wikimedia.org/wiki/File:A_Brazilian_family_in_Rio_de_Janeiro.jpg)

BASIC CONCEPTS

Meaning-making is an existentially relevant process that produces a surplus of *meaning*. Such a surplus triggers a demand for further meaning-making in an infinite process. This human feature makes life not a mere reaction to events but a constant future-oriented elaboration. We live in a world populated by things that are not just "things", people that are not just "people", and we ourselves barely feel we "are". The process of meaning-making allows us, on the one hand, to make sense of any expected or unexpected encounter – turning the extraordinary into the ordinary. On the other hand, it makes the life experience rich and alluring through the capacity to turn ordinary experiences and objects into extraordinary things (Marsico & Tateo, 2019) (Figure 1.9).

Figure 1.9 Coronation chair of Denmark by Bendix Grodtschilling, 1671 (https://commons.wikimedia.org/wiki/File:Coronation_Chair_Denmark_(King).jpg)

BASIC CONCEPTS

The coronation ceremony of the Danish kings between 1671 and 1840 used a particular type of throne. Frederik III ordered this chair from the craftsman Bendix Grodtschilling, inspired by the stories of King Solomon from the Old Testament. A rumour was spread about its legendary status: it was said that it was made of unicorn horn. In reality, it is made from narwhale tusks, a material the Danish kings could initially claim almost as their own because of the Danish ownership of Iceland and the Faroe islands. An object of mundane use (sitting) is turned into an extraordinary object by the basic act of decorating (Valsiner, 2018a) and by the production of a particular imaginative narrative (the unicorn). At the same time, the surplus of meaning attributed to the extraordinary object is used to normalize a particular state of affairs (the Danish dominion) into a "natural" condition.

The main process by which human beings produce, maintain, and demolish meanings is called *semiosis*. The elements involved in the process of semiosis are called *signs*. Through the production and interpretation of signs, human beings produce the surplus of meaning through which ordinary and extraordinary dimensions of the world feed into each other.

**GROUP ACTIVITY FOR INSTRUCTOR:
DIFFERENT TYPES OF SIGNS**

Start a group discussion by asking, "What do you think a sign is?". Collect a first round of answers and then ask the students to go outside the classroom for ten minutes and take a few pictures of what they consider "signs" in the environment. When they come back, ask them to show their pictures and explain why they chose to take each picture. It is important to make the students share the reasoning and rationale for the choice.

Reflection questions
1. What are signs made of?
2. What is NOT a sign?
3. If you see something for the first time, how do you know whether it is a sign or not?

Charles Sanders Peirce (1839–1914) was an American scientist, mathematician, logician, and philosopher.

SIGNS AND SEMIOSIS

Imagine being a palaeontologist looking for traces of the first species of hominids. You are excavating a site in a cave where the remains of a prehistoric settlement are supposed to be. Suddenly, you find a stone with a particular shape that makes you think about a possible archaeological discovery. How do you decide whether the stone is "just" a random stone, or is the product of hominids' activity? In the former case it will not mean much to you, in the latter it becomes archaeological evidence: an index of something that you are

BASIC CONCEPTS

looking for. This act is very common in everyday life, although most of the time we are not aware of it. It is called *interpretation*. When we perform an act of interpretation, we turn a thing into an object. This idea is based on the semiotic theory of C. S. Peirce (1839–1914): "By an object, I mean anything that we can think, i.e., anything we can talk about" (Peirce, MS [R] 966: Quoted in Olteanu: 2015: 261). Any "thing" can become a semiotic object, despite its attributes, like the materiality or the mode of existence, its being ordinary or extraordinary, its being concrete or abstract.

The process of production and interpretation of signs is called *semiosis*. According to Peirce, the emergence of mind is based on the process of semiosis, or, in other words, the mind is a specific form of semiosis. In general terms:

> A sign, or Representamen, is a First that stands in such a genuine triadic
> relation to a Second, called its Object, as to be capable of determining
> a Third, called its Interpretant, to assume the same triadic relation
> to its object in which it stands itself to the same object. The triadic
> relationship is genuine, that is its three members are bound together by it
> in a way that does not consist in any complex dyadic relation.
>
> (Peirce, CP 2.274)

The first element is that semiosis is based on triads (Figure 1.10). As we remember, dual systems do not allow development.

The sign is indeed made of a triplet in which two different elements are mediated by a third. This mediation provides both the "meaning" of the sign and the necessary degree of uncertainty to allow any form of development, for it implies the possibility of misunderstanding, misinterpretation, negotiation, and even deceiving. The second relevant element is that the triadic structure implies special relationships between the sub-parts. The elements composing the sign-system are indeed in relationships with *substitution*, *distinction*, *unification*, and *temporality*.

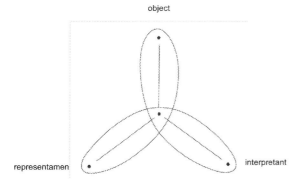

Figure 1.10 The sign system according to Peirce

1. *Substitution* because the representamen stands for its object.
2. *Distinction* because by logic the representamen cannot be the object it represents.
3. *Unification* because the semiotic production of the sign brings into the same whole elements that were not necessarily sub-parts of the triad before.
4. *Temporality* because semiosis takes place in irreversible time: something always turns into something else that turns into something else, etc. The process of interpretation is "governing facts in the future" (Peirce CP 1.23, 1903).

If you walk into a forest and spot some smoke between the trees: "A" (the smoke) stands for "B" (the fire: substitution) in some respect or capacity of a "C" (the interpretant, in this case the process of combustion). The smoke is not the fire (distinction), but it is also part of the same whole fire–combustion–smoke (unification). At any moment in the future, the sign or a sub-part can turn into another element of a new sign (temporality).

> The representamen may be a cloud of smoke that suddenly appears over a cluster of silver-tipped spruce in the Rocky Mountain National Park in Colorado. A Ranger spies the sign. Immediately a semiotic object, fire, comes to mind. Then there is an interpretant that mediates and brings the representamen and semiotic object together to create the concept of a dangerous situation that demands immediate action. The Ranger calls for help, and moves in for a closer look. There's the fire! The semiotic object suddenly becomes the representamen whose semiotic object points toward the physical destruction that the flames are wreaking on the natural habitat. A quickly constructed interpretant tells the Ranger that the condition is more severe than she had originally suspected. The apparent danger, from her original interpretant, becomes a representamen that provokes a semiotic object involving a nearby campground. An interpretant involving danger comes into the picture.
> (Merrell, 2001, p. 30)

Every sign can become a representamen of a new system, in a chain of interpretation that is potentially infinite but actually bounded by contextual elements such as habits, culture, etc.

The third important aspect to keep in mind is Peirce's classification of signs. There are different ways in which the elements of the triad can be related: they are called *index*, *icon*, and *symbol* (Figure 1.11).

In the index, the representamen has some actual physical connection with its object (the smoke is linked to the fire by a physical causal connection). In the icon, the representamen has some similarity or analogical resemblance with its object but not a physical connection (the signal representing some

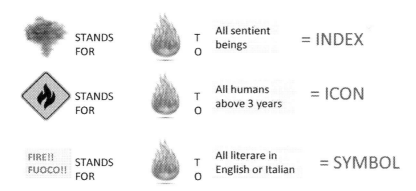

Figure 1.11 Classification of signs

abstract flames). Finally, the representamen in the symbol has only an arbitrary relationship with its object, and this is established by social convention (the sequence of letters f–i–r–e holds no causal relationship with the object "fire", but in a given community of speakers, the convention of using the sequence of letters to refer to that object has been established).

The three types of signs imply different relations with the type of agents that can interpret them. An index can be potentially interpreted by any sentient being (even some plants can react to smoke and fire by eliciting a response, like pines letting their cones fall to the ground). To interpret an icon, the agent requires a minimum of specific competence, a minimum of learning, so the audience of potential interpreters is smaller. Any primate or human being above 2–3 years, no matter from which part of the world, can learn to interpret a signal as meaning "fire". A symbol is for a more restricted "elite" of interpreters. To understand the meaning of an arbitrary relationship between representamen, object, and interpretant, one needs to be socialized in a specific cultural community (even some special signs like onomatopoeias are not completely iconic and the conventions change according to cultures: a dog barks "woof" in the USA and "bau" in Italy).

Yet the capability to interpret symbols does not constrain the capability to interpret other types of signs. Besides, if the mind is a semiotic process, the signs will play a role under the three forms, not just as symbols.

> Human communities unfortunately place undue priority on the symbolic mode. The human tendency is to 'linguicize' (symbolize) all signs. This tendency has become endemic in our increasingly wordy cultures. Yet, in the affairs of everyday life, all three sign types, icons, indices, and symbols, never cease to make their presence known. [. . .] *We live in a world of icons and indices more than a world of words (symbols).*
> (Merrel, 2001, pp. 34–35, original emphasis)

Figure 1.12 A brand logo in which iconic and symbolic elements feed into each other to reinforce and orient towards a desired interpretation (https://commons.wikimedia.org/wiki/File:Thee_%27Peacock_Brand%27,_Otto_Roelofs_%26_Zoonen,_Amsterdam.JPG)

Indeed, any linguistic sign also has an iconic dimension, while any icon also has a symbolic one. This is a very basic concept embedded in several human activities, such as religion and marketing (Figure 1.12).

SIGNS AND MEANING-MAKING

Signs are powerful tools of transformation. Human beings use them to attribute surplus of meaning to objects, other people, and experiences. Cultural psychology is particularly interested in those phenomena of collective everyday life – such as fashion, rituals, and food – in which signs are used to produce surplus meaning to turn, for example, ordinary pieces of clothing (Figure 1.13A) into extraordinary objects of fashion (Figure 1.13B) (Marsico & Tateo, 2019; Valsiner, 2018a).

The interaction between signs and other objects is powerful enough to change even the ontological status of a particular object (Figure 1.14).

A simple apple can be appreciated as a natural food, yet the simple act of sticking a sign on it turns the apple into "non-nature", which entails the possibility of selling it and thus turning it into a *commodity*. Even if the material qualities of the apple – its origin, its chemical composition, its ripeness – do not change, its meaning is changed by using a particular symbol (the logo). The power of signs is so great that one would probably be ready to say that the *branded* apple tastes better. So, it seems that signs play some role in the way human beings experience the world.

Lev Semyonovich Vygotsky (1896–1934) was a Soviet psychologist, the founder of a theory of human cultural and bio-social development commonly referred to as cultural–historical psychology.

BASIC CONCEPTS

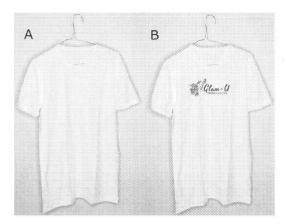

Figure 1.13 Signs and objects

Figure 1.14 A sign can turn nature into a commodity

MEDIATION

Some animal species – birds, apes, etc. including humans – exhibit some form of practical thinking. They can use an object or some indirect procedure to solve a practical problem, such as reaching food beyond their limbs' range. In some cases, this capability is inscribed in instinctual schemes (animals are born with it), sometimes it is acquired through learning and imitation (adults show the young, who can imitate with their own variations). The American psychologist James Mark Baldwin (1894) theorized that imitation is not just a mimesis of observed behavior. He surmised the importance of the process of "persistent imitation" in the development of human consciousness. Indeed, "in the constant exercise of imitation, new adaptations are acquired" (Baldwin, 1894, p. 35). The idea of persistent imitation has long been forgotten (Valsiner, 2018b), although it represents a first insight into the process of internalization of signs. According to Baldwin (1894), the child begins by

25

James Mark Baldwin (1861–1934) was an American philosopher and psychologist. He proposed innovative ideas in developmental and social psychology that would later be adopted by Janet, Lacan, Bateson, and Valsiner.

imitating an observed behavior, but each repetition becomes progressively more distanced from the original model, which may no longer be available as a stimulus. In other words, the child progressively imitates her own behaviour and each repetition is also a creative variation (Valsiner, 2018b).

> The child reproduces the copy thus obtained, consisting of the physical signs and, through them, of the mental accompaniments. By this reproduction it 'interprets' its projects as subjective in itself, and then refers them back to the 'other person' again.
>
> (Baldwin, 1894, p. 43)

Through persistent imitation, the developing child progressively distances herself from the sensory data and *appropriates* the behaviour by creating her own version of the original stimulus, which remains available as a memory.

This is a very important aspect of animal life and it signals that complex living beings do not rely only on their perceptual–motor capabilities to relate to the world. Sometimes, they put *something* between themselves and the world: a mediation. This is particularly relevant for human beings, whose experience of the world and action upon it is completely mediated by something. This axiom is the starting point of the so-called cultural–historical theory, based on Karl Marx philosophy, which assumes that human beings actively produce and modify their world through collectively coordinated labor (Vygotsky & Luria, 1994). In doing so, they use resources beyond brute muscular force. They use tools that mediate their relationship with the material world and with other human beings (Gillespie & Zittoun, 2010; Ma, 2014; Vygotsky & Luria, 1994). According to Vygotsky and Luria (1994), the use of mediation tools in practical intellectual tasks is not the qualitative leap that distinguished humans from other animals. The turning point is when the infant human acquires the capability of managing a particular type of mediation tool: something we already know as a *symbol*.

> The great genetic moment of all intellectual development, from which grew the purely human forms of practical and gnostic intellect, is realized in the unification of these two previously completely independent lines of development. The child's use of tools is comparable to that of an ape's only during the former's pre-speech period. As soon as speech and the use of symbolic signs are included in this operation, it transforms itself along entirely new lines, overcoming the former natural laws and for the first time giving birth to authentically human use of implements. From the moment the child begins to master the situation with the help of speech, after mastering his own behaviour, a radically new organization of behaviour appears, as well as new relations with the environment. We are witnessing the birth of those specifically human forms of behaviour that, breaking away from animal forms of

behaviour, later create intellect and go on to become the base of labour: the specifically human form of the use of tools.

(Vygotsky & Luria, 1994, pp. 108–109)

The most powerful, ubiquitous, and flexible mediation tool based on signs in human beings is language. From a certain point onwards in infant development, humans acquire the capability of managing linguistic symbols to regulate the relationship with the world (and other people), and later to use signs on themselves. From a certain moment in development, "the child solves a practical task with the help of not only eyes and hands, but also speech" (Vygotsky & Luria, 1994, pp. 109). Since that moment, the power of symbolic mediation becomes overarching among the psychological functions, to the point that experience is organized through linguistic categories. In sum, meaning-making is produced through semiosis, that is the use and interpretation of signs. Signs mediate the relationship with the world and the psychological experiences. But signs are produced, maintained, and demolished in the context of collective coordinated activities. The use of signs does not exist outside a community of people sharing those very signs.

Jerome Seymour Bruner (1915–2016) was an American psychologist who innovated psychological sciences in different moments. He started the so-called *Cognitive Revolution* in the 1960s; was one of the founders of cultural psychology in the 1980s; and one of the beginners of the *narrative turn in psychology* in the 1990s.

ACTIVITY AND ARTIFACT

When we are born, we encounter a world that pre-exists us. We are born in a place (a house, a hospital, etc.) where two or more people are waiting for us, having made particular arrangements to facilitate the process. That particular *activity* called *child delivery* can take different forms in different parts of the world. However, no matter how it looks, it will involve collective coordinated action with the use of some tools and some procedures (and rituals) to achieve a shared goal. Language mediation will play an important role in coordinating people action, anticipating the events, fixing problems, and making sense of what happens. Someone will probably ask "Is it a boy or a girl?" and maybe provice some specific items (clothing, amulets, medicines, etc.), following a shared belief or a story about how to make an infant healthy.

> We live in a sea of stories, and like the fish who (according to the proverb) will be the last to discover water, we have our own difficulties grasping what it is like to swim in stories. It is not that we lack competence in creating our narrative accounts of reality – far from it. We are, if anything, too expert. Our problem, rather, is achieving consciousness of what we so easily do automatically, the ancient problem of *prise de conscience* (becoming aware).
>
> (Bruner, 1996, p. 147)

Most of the mundane activities we entertain share this characteristic: they appear so natural and habitual that we forget how much they are the result of a historical process that was constructed them over time, with local variations; thanks to the contribution of different people and the use of different tools; and codified to be transmitted through stories, manuals, and rituals. Thus, human beings participate to shared and socially organized *activities* (Wertsch, 1981). They do not ingest food; they have breakfast and lunch. They do not clean themselves; they take a shower or a bath. They do not mate; they have an affair or a marriage. The term *activity* was used by Soviet psychologists to describe practical and intellectual action stimulated by a particular motive, subordinated to a particular goal, and organized according to shared rules (Wertsch, 1981). All human life is thus framed in a context of activity that mediates the personal experience by, for instance, suggesting the proper, acceptable, or habitual way of running that activity.

If one puts together the concepts of mediation, semiosis, and activity, one realizes that the core idea is that human beings construct their version of the world in their doings. Indeed, according to Vygotsky and the cultural–historical theory, the human being is *Homo Faber*, the making human. The human living environment is the outcome of an active process of production: it is an *artifact*. According to Michael Cole,

> an artifact is an aspect of the material world that has been modified over the history of its incorporation into goal-directed human action. By virtue of the changes wrought in the process of their creation and use, artifacts are simultaneously ideal (conceptual) and material. They are ideal in that their material form has been shaped by their participation in the interactions of which they were previously a part and which they mediate in the present.
>
> (Cole, 2003, p. 117)

The whole planet Earth is nowadays so affected by human activities that the whole world has been modified by human activity to some extent. The Earth almost turned into an artifact, to the point that scientists named a new geological era the *Anthropocene* (Davies, 2016).

Artifacts are the product of shared human activity over time. Thus, any material object (e.g., a stone, a piece of wood, etc.) can turn into an artifact once it is used in a certain way for a certain purpose in the context of an activity. Going back to the example of the palaeontologist who needs to decide whether a stone is an archaeological finding, the question is the capability to identify *signs* of human activity that marked the object and to interpret those signs in the correct way.

The variety of human activities has created a wide range of artifacts, both material and non-material. Artifacts can also be categorized according to the level of abstraction in relation to the activity.

1. Primary artifacts, intuitively, are those directly used in production (e.g. hammers, pens, computers, but also words and music notes).

2. Secondary artifacts are the "instructions" for the use of primary artifacts. They are the representations of primary artifacts and of modes of action using primary artifacts (e.g. recipes, traditional beliefs, norms, constitutions, manuals).
3. Tertiary artifacts constitute the most abstract level and the one that is easy to consider transparent and "natural". Those are the artifacts that talk about the other levels or suggest "why" and "when" it is appropriate to use the artifacts.

> In modern psychological jargon, modes of behavior acquired when interacting with tertiary artifacts can transfer beyond the immediate contexts of their use. [. . .] works of art and processes, of perception; [. . .] notions of schemas and scripts and [. . .] notions of context, mediation, and activity found in contemporary cognitive psychology, anthropology, and allied parts of the cognitive sciences.
>
> (Cole, 2003, p. 122)

The levels do not necessarily correspond to different artifacts. As in the case of a sign that can include different functions (iconic, symbolic, etc.), in the case of an artifact the different levels are present and feed into each other. Take for instance the t-shirt in Figure 1.13B. As a primary artifact, the t-shirt has some characteristics derived from a history of production and use (the color, the shape, the fabric, etc.) that afford it participation in some activities (dressing). At the secondary level, the artifact involves some rules of use (e.g., there is one inside and one outside, you must first buy it and possibly not shoplift it, etc.). The secondary level is of course affected by the primary (the inside is determined by the production technique). At the tertiary level one can find the imaginative and artistic aspects of the artifact (being a branded piece of clothing) that affect its material qualities (the price). In return, the primary qualities of the artifact (color, fabric) affect its rules of use and its tertiary characteristics (one should not wear it at a formal ceremony).

An artifact such as the t-shirt in Figure 1.13B mediates the person's experience in the goal-oriented activity (Figure 1.15).

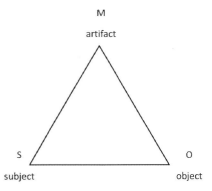

Figure 1.15 The basic mediational triangle

The process is usually represented by the minimal mediational triangle (Figure 1.15) in which subject and object are not only "directly" connected but, simultaneously, "indirectly" connected through a medium constituted of artifacts (Cole, 2023). The mediated path is typically that of culture, which can be understood as a collection of artifacts and doings shared by a given community in a historical period. The direct and the mediated paths are not mutually exclusive – they are complementary. "The emergence of mediated action does not mean that the mediated path replaces the natural one, just as the appearance of culture in phylogeny does not mean that culture replaces phylogeny" (Cole, 2023, p. 119).

The typical metaphor to describe the synergy between mediated and non-mediated psychological functioning is that of cultivation.

> Developmental propensity emerges from subjects' social practice in their social situations, and the propensity strives to evolve and realize itself in the real social situation, which constitutes the realistic vision and background for educational guidance: educational efforts have to learn to deal with this strong subjective force in its continuously evolving process.
>
> (Wu, Xu & Li, 2021, p. 13)

One can understand human development as a process of cultivation, in which repeated actions taking place in a context with environmental conditions (a type of soil, sunlight, etc.), by using mediation tools (the gardening tools), indirectly affect the development of the organism (watering, fertilizing, etc.) in a balance between the organism's ontogenetic features (an apple tree will never produce bananas), the affordances of the environment (the social relations in the case of humans), and the desired developmental goal (Vygotsky, 1997). It is now clear that cultural psychology considers the person and the environment as inseparable units and aims to understand their mutual relationships. How does the environment feed into the psyche and vice versa?

FROM THE WORLD TO THE PSYCHE AND BACK: THE INTERNALIZATION/EXTERNALIZATION CYCLE

Very early in their development, human beings learn that there is a difference between what happens inside themselves and what happens outside, including other humans and animate or inanimate beings. "Differentiation is a major formal property of an organismic system" (Witkin, Goodenough & Oltman, 1979, p. 1127). At the same time, developing human beings must learn how to establish healthy relationships between those apparently separate worlds. According to the psychologist Kurt Lewin (1942), the child experiences a psychological environment which is boundless, made of objects and persons that are somehow part of his own individuality.

> [T]he newborn cannot distinguish between himself and his environment; slowly certain areas, for instance, those connected with eating, take on specific character, become more and more differentiated; the parts of his own body become differentiated from each other and from the rest of the world; social relations develop and become differentiated; needs, emotions, language go through a similar process of differentiation.
>
> (Lewin 1942, p. 226)

Kurt Lewin (1890–1947) was a German psychologist, interested in developmental processes, famous for his *field theory*. When he emigrated to the USA before WWI he became one of the modern pioneers of social, organizational, and applied psychology.

This life space is also timeless, as the infant lives in present time; and it is magically real, in the sense that the boundary between real and unreal is blurry. The child's life space progressively differentiates through social experiences and encounters with people and objects, and new parts are formed, new configurations emerge.

Cultural psychology shares the axiom that psychological functions are generated by social experiences, by a child's participation in collective activities. According to Vygotsky, higher psychological functions are internalized social relationships. He formalized the idea in a *general genetic law of cultural development*:

> The most important and basic of genetic laws, to which the study of the higher psychological functions leads us, reads that every symbolic activity of the child was once a social form of co-operation and preserves throughout its development, to its highest point, the social method of its functioning. The history of the higher psychological functions is disclosed here as the history of the transformation of means of social behaviour into means of individual psychological organization.
>
> (Vygotsky & Luria, 1994, p. 138)

The principle of *sociogenesis* is quite simple: from a very early age, infants are involved in social interactions with adults and peers. The social relationships require a process of meaning-making, generating messages that are internalized (they require active work on interpretation and response) by the person. This process is of course mediated and the meaning is produced (not merely reproduced) by the person. Through the repeated participation in social relationships, a function that first appeared as interpersonal (e.g., language) is progressively internalized and appropriated by the child. In other words, the child learns how to use it as an artifact, which generates a new psychological function that makes the psychological system more differentiated. Once the new function is managed, the child can use it autonomously in new interpsychic relations (Figure 1.21). The first mediation tool that an infant encounters through social interactions during the first year of life is the caregiver.

From the second month of life, the infant engages in coordinated interactions with the caregiver that play a critical role in development. Through

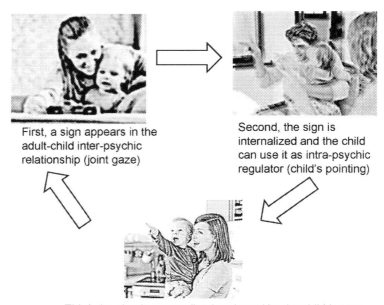

First, a sign appears in the adult-child inter-psychic relationship (joint gaze)

Second, the sign is internalized and the child can use it as intra-psychic regulator (child's pointing)

Third, the sign is externalized and used by the child in new inter-psychic relationships, enabling the participation to more sophisticated social interactions (child's asking mother to reach a distant object).

Figure 1.16 The internalization/externalization cycle of sign mediation

repeated dyadic coordination of vocalization, gaze behavior, and (later) joint deictics, the infant develops the capability to participate in social interactions and to regulate pragmatically her own and other's conduct (Northrup & Iverson, 2020). Once the sign produced during the coordinated interactions is internalized, the infant learns that the other can become, for instance, an extension of her own body to reach a distant object if the proper signs are produced (third step in Figure 1.16).

According to Valsiner (2014), each cycle of internalization/externalization implies a personalization of the meaning of the social interaction that is partially shared by the participants. In other words, one does not passively receive the meanings produced in social interactions. One reinterprets and personalizes those messages, responding in a new version of those meanings.

In conclusion, the person's psychological system and the environment do not merely mirror each other. Neither do they exist as independent. They exist as parts of a person/environment whole, feeding into each other. According to cultural psychology, there is no human being outside a social context, just as there cannot be any superindividual social dimension without the contribution of a person. For human beings, the world and the psyche constitute each other in a mutual relationship where both are at the same time product and producer of the other.

BASIC CONCEPTS

> **SUMMARY OF CHAPTER 1**
>
> In Chapter 1, we have started to become familiar with the fundamental concepts and processes that are shared by the different approaches of cultural psychology.
>
> The concept of *cogenetic logic* states that the experience of the world as well as the concepts that describe it at abstract level are organized in a triadic system. The concept "A" can be understood only in relation to its logical negation "non-A" and the boundary conditions that put them in relation.
>
> The process of *meaning-making* is the main activity of the human mind. Meaning is constantly produced, maintained, and sometimes demolished to make sense of experiences and to govern the uncertainty of the future.
>
> Meaning is produced through *semiosis*, that is the activity of production and interpretation of signs. *Signs* are elements that living beings can use to regulate their own and others' intellectual and practical behavior.
>
> Human beings have the characteristic of being part of historical social communities whose members share coordinated *activities*. This pre-existing context involves the use of *artifacts*, both material and immaterial objects (such as signs) that *mediate* the action and the relationships. The *context of activity* frames the person's experience and suggests habitual ways of doing things.
>
> Finally, coordination and integration between the psychic system and the environment is ensured by *cycles of internalization/externalization*. The meanings produced in inter-psychic social relations are first internalized and mastered by the person in the form of new psychic functions. Afterwards, the person is able to use again those meanings in new and more complex social interactions.
>
> Once we have acquired the basic bricks, we can move to the conceptual building of cultural psychology. In the next chapter, we will read about its history and theories.

Check your knowledge and reflect

Task: Choose an everyday activity that you can observe (e.g., using public transport; attending school; going to a restaurant; etc.) and try to identify the signs, artifacts, agents, schedules, norms, values, etc. involved by using the concepts described in this chapter. Write a short essay (maximum two pages; you can include images that you take) elaborating your personal view and using the concepts presented so far. Then, share your essay with two colleagues and ask for their feedback.

REFERENCES

Baldwin, J. M. (1894). Imitation: A chapter in the natural history of consciousness. *Mind, 3*(9), 26–55.

Bruner, J. S. (1996). *The culture of education*. Cambridge, MA: Harvard University Press.

Cole, M. (2003). *Cultural psychology: A once and future discipline*, 6th edition. Cambridge, MA: Harvard University Press.

Davies, J. (2016). *The birth of the Anthropocene*. Oakland, CA: University of California Press.

Frankl, V. E. (2010). *The feeling of meaninglessness: A challenge to psychotherapy and philosophy*. (D. Hallowell, Trans.). Milwaukee, WI: Marquette University Press.

Gillespie, A., & Zittoun, T. (2010). Using resources: Conceptualizing the mediation and reflective use of tools and signs. *Culture & Psychology, 16*(1), 37–62. https://doi.org/10.1177/1354067x09344888

Herbst, P. G. (2012). *Alternatives to hierarchies (Vol. 1)*. New York: Springer Science & Business Media. https://doi.org/10.1007/978-1-4684-6945-5

Kullasepp, K., & Marsico, G. (Eds.). (2021). *Identity at the borders and between the borders*. Cham: Springer International Publishing. https://doi.org/10.1007/978-3-030-62267-1

Lewin, K. (1942). Field theory and learning. In N. B. Henry (Ed.), *The forty-first yearbook of the national society for the study of education* (pp. 215–242). Bloomington, IN: Public School Publishing Company.

Ma, J. (2014). The synergy of Peirce and Vygotsky as an analytical approach to the multimodality of semiotic mediation. *Mind, Culture, and Activity, 21*(4), 374–389. https://doi.org/10.1080/10749039.2014.913294

Marsico, G., & Tateo, L. (Eds.). (2019). *Ordinary things and their extraordinary meanings*. Charlotte, NC: IAP.

Merrell, F. (2001). Charles Sanders Peirce's concept of the sign. In P. Cobley (Ed.), *The Routledge companion to semiotics and linguistics* (pp. 28–39). London: Routledge.

Northrup, J. B., & Iverson, J. M. (2020). The development of mother–infant coordination across the first year of life. *Developmental Psychology, 56*(2), 221–236. https://doi.org/10.1037/dev0000867

Olteanu, A. (2015). *Philosophy of education in the semiotics of Charles Peirce: A cosmology of learning and loving*. Oxford: Peter Lang.

Peirce, C. S. (1931–1958). *Collected papers of Charles Sanders Peirce*. Cambridge, MA: Harvard University Press.

Tateo, L. (2016). Toward a cogenetic cultural psychology. *Culture & Psychology, 22*(3), 433–447. https://doi.org/10.1177/1354067X16645297

Tateo, L. (2020). The golem of psychology and the ecosystemic epistemology. *Integrative Psychological and Behavioral Science*, 54, 667–676. https://doi.org/10.1007/s12124-020-09532-5

Tateo, L., & Marsico, G. (2021). Signs as borders and borders as signs. *Theory & Psychology, 31*(5), 708–728. https://doi.org/10.1177/0959354320964865

Truffaut, F., & Hitchcock, A. (1985). *Hitchcock*. New York: Simon & Schuster.

Valsiner J. (2014). *An invitation to cultural psychology*, London: Sage. https://doi.org/10.4135/9781473905986

Valsiner, J. (2018a). *Ornamented lives*. Charlotte, NC: IAP.

Valsiner, J. (2018b). Roots of creativity: Variability amplification through persistent imitation. In T. Zittoun & V. Glăveanu (Eds.), *Handbook of imagination and culture* (pp. 47–60). Oxford: Oxford University Press.

Vygotsky, L.S. (1997) *Educational psychology*. Boca Raton, FL: St. Lucie Press (Originally written 1921–1923).

Vygotsky, L.S., & Luria, A. (1994). Tool and symbol in child development. In R. Van de Veer & J. Valsiner (Eds.), *The Vygotsky reader* (pp. 99–174). Oxford: Oxford University Press.

Webster, D., & Kruglanski, A. (1994). Individual differences in need for cognitive closure. *Journal of Personality and Social Psychology*, *67*(6), 1049–1062. https://doi.org/10.1037/0022-3514.67.6.1049

Wertsch, J. V. (1981). *The concept of activity in Soviet psychology*. New York: Sharpe.

Witkin, H. A., Goodenough, D. R., & Oltman, P. K. (1979). Psychological differentiation: Current status. *Journal of Personality and Social Psychology*, *37*(7), 1127–1145. https://doi.org/10.1037/0022-3514.37.7.1127

Wu, A., Xu, S., & Li, X. (2021). Transforming by following forces: Introducing Chinese philosophy of SHI and SHUN SHI into developmental and educational psychology. *Culture & Psychology*, *27*(3), 359–373. https://doi.org/10.1177/1354067X211017302

CHAPTER 2

The forms of knowing

Scan the QR-code to access additional materials and watch outstanding international scholars discussing key concepts.

> **LEARNING GOALS**
>
> 1. To understand the forms of knowledge produced in cultural psychology
> 2. To learn the basic ways of producing knowledge (methodology) in cultural psychology
> 3. To learn how to introduce developmental focus in psychological sciences

CHAPTER OVERVIEW

In this chapter, we discuss the characteristics of cultural psychology's methodology. Starting with the epistemological principles (what type of knowledge), we will discuss the methodological principles (how do we produce knowledge). The focus of cultural psychology is always on the genesis and development of human psychological phenomena that unfold in time and space, in relation to others but in a unique personal form. Thus, we will first discuss the concepts of temporality, dialogicality, and narrativity and how they shape our common knowledge. Finally, we will present some of the fundamental principles of the qualitative methodology to produce knowledge in cultural psychology.

GROUP ACTIVITY FOR THE INSTRUCTOR: THE LETTER

The task for the group is to write a letter to their child self. The students can write a half page letter addressing their younger self in a particularly significant moment of their childhood. They can for instance talk about their present selves, give advice to the younger self, etc. The students have about 15 minutes to complete the first task. Then the instructor asks the students to write another half page with the reply of the younger self to the adult. This will take 15 minutes more. The instructor will then invite the students to a group discussion to share the experience and ask them questions about how they reacted to the different perspectives, how they felt, what types of reflection they made.

Reflection questions

The purpose of the activity is to produce an artifact by which the student can establish an inner dialogue between different I-positions. The topics to reflect are temporality, irreversibility of time, pace of development, turning points, inner dialogue, and using different internalized voices.

1. How did you feel writing to yourself?
2. Did you use the words of other significant persons (e.g., your parents)?
3. How did you experience the passage of time?

The purpose of doing research in cultural psychology is to make *accessible and visible the process of meaning-making*. Most of psychology is concerned with the observation, explanation, prediction, and control of observable individual behavior. But behavior is a temporary, selective, and superficial aspect of human psychology. The *absence* of behavior, although not directly observable with traditional psychological methods, is as much relevant as the *presence* of behavior. For instance, seldom has research been interested in apparent "refraining" from behavior. In cultural psychology, Olga Lehmann, for instance, studied *silence* as a form of meaning-making (Lehmann, 2016). In Chapter 1, we discussed how meaning-making is produced through *semiosis*, which is the production and interpretation of different types of signs. Thus, the way of studying psychological phenomena in cultural psychology must be able to grasp the visible and invisible use of different types of signs by the person interacting with the surroundings in irreversible time.

TEMPORALITY

All human phenomena happen at a certain moment in time and in a certain place. Temporality is thus a characteristic of all the phenomena psychology is interested in (Simão, Guimarães & Valsiner, 2015). This is something we take for granted and so we overlook it. According to Kant (1986), time and space are the fundamental principles on which we organize our knowledge of the world. But there is also a more mundane, yet not banal, meaning of this idea. Human phenomena happen at a certain time and in a certain place, which makes them unique in their characteristics. A person born in Italy in the 15th century would never be replicable or similar to a person born in the same place but in the 20th century. This means that the fact of happening in that *very* place at that *very* time is part of the unique characteristics of a phenomenon – it is not incidental. This also means that once something happens in a certain time/space it cannot be undone: time is irreversible. This apparently trivial aspect is often ignored in psychology and in many social sciences, which act as if unique phenomena could be treated as similar even if they happen to different persons at different moments (Valsiner, 2017). Drawing from the Theory of Relativity in physics, Mikhail Bakhtin (1981) claimed that space/time is part of the things we say (or the stories we write) and they form a whole. Unlike Kant, time and space do not pre-exist experience, they are rather an inherent part of what happens. Bakhtin called this concept *chronotope* (1981), and it is central to human meaning-making and thus for cultural psychology.

Mikhail Mikhailovich Bakhtin (1895–1975) was a Russian philosopher, literary critic, and scholar who worked on literary theory, ethics, and the philosophy of language.

The principle of temporality has an existential and a methodological consequence. From the existential point of view, the simple fact that life proceeds in one direction – from birth to death – creates an asymmetry in the value of time. "This is an inevitable condition for all organisms that flourish within irreversible time – we can only look forward to tomorrow, but we cannot re-live yesterday" (Valsiner, 2014, p. 7). The methodological consequence is that one needs to consider the concrete spatio-temporal conditions in which a phenomenon occurs in order to understand it.

IRREVERSIBLE TIME

Valsiner (2014) introduced the axiomatic principle that all life events make sense in the flow of irreversible time. In psychology, time is often considered

THE FORMS OF KNOWING

Hans Adolf Eduard Driesch (1867–1941) was a German biologist and philosopher. He is most noted for his early experimental work in embryology and for his neo-vitalist philosophy of entelechy.

a secondary aspect and it is often understood in terms of point-like events. For instance, in empirical psychology, data must be produced *here and now*, preferably in the presence of the researcher, to be considered valid. In dynamic psychology, the past is the causal force that determines the present state of affairs. If a researcher wants to introduce a longitudinal dimension or time as independent variable in a study, time is usually conceptualized as a succession of static moments (T_0-----T_1-----T_2......T_N). The principle of *irreversible time* states instead that life flows in a single direction and it is not possible to go back. Thus, time is a continuous flow that moves from *past* to *future* and human beings identify some specific events on this flow that they define as the *present*. Such a mundane observation has tremendous implications:

> I never *can* have the very same content a second or third time, because, by its having been had already, it is made different from what it was the first time! For the second or any subsequent time, that content carries in itself two accents: one of *before* and another of *already known*, which it did not carry when it was possessed first. Thus every content is exclusively what it is and there *cannot* be two quite identical contents.
> (Driesch, 1925, p. 25, emphasis in original)

Thus, treating two different events as similar is an abstraction that serves to organize experience, but does not correspond to an ontological reality. In cultural psychology, this implies that irreversible time must become part of any theoretical or methodological move (Figure 2.1).

For instance, a longitudinal research design would consider the measurements at T_1 and T_2 as equivalent to the situations measured at T_3 and T_4 because they have been measured at quantitatively determined distances. However, T_1 is not equivalent to T_2 or T_4, because T_2 includes the history of

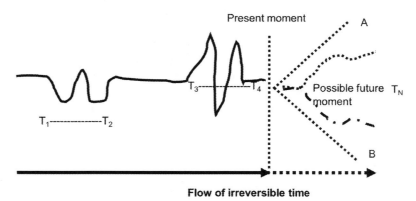

Figure 2.1 Irreversible time affects the way psychology understands the phenomena

40

T_1, and T_4 includes the past history of T_1 to T_3. On the contrary, T_1 does not include the history of T_2 or T_4. So, despite treating all T intervals as quantitatively equivalent, they represent phenomena that are *qualitatively* different.[1] Besides, what can be called the present, is nothing other than the latest one of the points (T_N) in time in which one observes a phenomenon. The phenomenon itself will continue to develop in an open future, in which potentially unfolding directions (A and B in Figure 2.1) are only partially constrained but not determined by the past trajectory.

If one combines the principle of *irreversible time* with the concept of *semiosis*, it is possible to understand how human beings – in the inter(action) with their environment – produce signs that operate in irreversible time (Figure 2.2) (Valsiner, 2014).

In Valsiner's own words:

> Within the flow of the irreversible time, the sign (S) differentiates from the ongoing experience and becomes available at the present moment to guide that moment towards the future in two ways: immediately (at the locus of the Act), and through its relative extension over time – for the future (Sf). The act of meaningful social construction is thus always dual, involving action towards the future through the context of the sign (S), and vice versa (i.e. the sign has the act as its context).
>
> (Valsiner, 2014, p. 116)

"The *function of signs is always future-oriented*" (Valsiner, 2014, p. 117). A sign sets up a constraint (or a potentiality), turning the next immediate future into a new present and excluding some alternatives. For instance, if I say "I just got lunch" during a conversation at the present moment (a statement about a past event), I constrain the range of potential actions in the next future. It will sound awkward if I invite you for dinner immediately

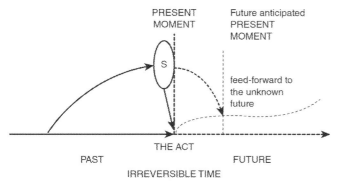

Figure 2.2 Semiosis in irreversible time (Valsiner, 2014, p. 117)

afterward. On the contrary, it will sound perfectly natural if I say something like "I am taking a nap".

Moreover, signs constrain the general orientation towards encountering similar situations in some future moment (promoting or inhibiting one of the future trajectories "A" or "B" in Figure 2.1) (Valsiner, 2014). The whole history of events from the past to the present moment (T_1 to T_4) represents the context of the phenomenon and cannot be separated from it.

Although it is apparently abstract, the axiom of irreversible time is crucial to the understanding of human experience. Countless human activities are constructed for the celebration of life moments that are made unique by the irreversible flow of time. We celebrate the first word of a child, the first day of school, the first kiss, the first time we make love, the first day of the year, etc. because we assume that they will be qualitatively different from the following ones. The existential experience of irreversible time contributes to producing a surplus of meaning for otherwise ordinary events of life.

TIME AS CONTEXT

Time is thus part of any phenomenon, and the forms of knowledge production must incorporate it into their methods. In the history of psychology, time has been accounted in different ways (Figure 2.3).

For instance, evolutionary theories, such as Darwin's or Haeckel's accounted only for biological time of the species' evolution. The individual ontogenetic development becomes an epiphenomenon of its belonging to a given species. Other theories, such as Piaget's and Freud's, focus on the individual ontogenetic and psychological time that allow the unfolding of biological development. The historic–cultural theories and the ecological theories instead take into account the psychological and cultural levels

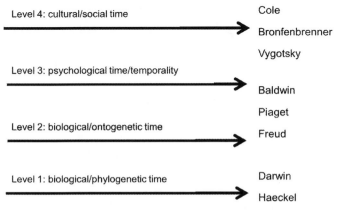

Figure 2.3 How psychology accounts for the different temporal levels

of time. Time as socially constructed in collective activities affects individual development. People attribute meaning to developmental transitions and milestones based on social–cultural guidance (Tateo & Valsiner, 2015). The four levels are of course an abstraction constructed in the specific cultural context of European philosophy. So, Piaget's theory of developmental stages can be generalized for human development in a specific culture – the 19th-century Swiss-Mittel European culture – but is questionable in a different cultural context (Tisdall et al., 2023). Thus, how time is accounted for in the methodology of cultural psychology?

The temporal dimension in cultural psychology is always *developmental* and *genetic*, in the sense that it considers the current observed phenomenon in relation to the historical development from its genesis to its possible future directions.

> The now does not exist on its own but exists only in relationship to the retention of past events and the expectations of future events that constitute the contextualizing perspective in relationship to which it can be noticed, the background by negation of which it can stand out. Now, in other words is always the now of a larger now.
>
> (Russon, 1998, p. 17)

Reflection question: What dimensions of time do you want to include in your research? How can you grasp those dimensions using a method?

All the levels of temporality in Figure 2.3 are present in human experience, although their distance from individual experience is different. For instance, there is a subjective and intimate experience of time with its accelerations and decelerations, with more or less arbitrary segmentation (Figure 2.4). There is an intersubjective level, related to the interaction and consensual construction of time and the regulation of coordinated activities, as when you invite your partner to a romantic dinner.

There is a socio-cultural level of time, regulating the societal practices and artifacts that mediate the intra-personal and intersubjective experience,

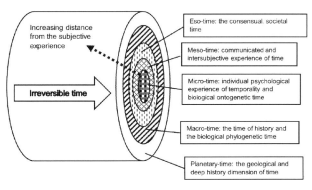

Figure 2.4 Time as context model

such as date and clock time. For instance, *dinner* with a partner can seldom occur at nine o'clock in the morning. There is a wider temporal context with a cultural–historical frame in which experience occurs. Finally, there is a planetary time that operates on a more-than-human timescale and that we seldom acknowledge in everyday life (Chakrabarty, 2021). For instance, the planetary timescale is the focus of evolutionary psychology, and it has also become central for the theorizing of environmental psychology. All the temporal levels contribute to the definition of temporal flow and to the construction of the relationship between past, present, and future.

Cultural psychology tries to understand the interaction between different temporal dimensions in human experience (Tateo & Valsiner, 2015). The individual temporality is affected by the socio-cultural time way before the actual moment of birth; for instance, the medical practices determine the duration and the practice of delivery (Bastos, Valsiner & Uriko, 2012). All human life course takes place in the context of different temporalities that frame and affect each other (Zittoun et al., 2013). Even an apparently serendipitous event such as establishing a couple relationship involves a complex interaction between subjective experiences of time: interpersonal temporal coordination (both person feeling it is "the right moment"); and the socio-cultural temporal guidance (what is the "right" temporal pace of a couple in each society). All those temporalities frame the unique genesis of a couple, their shared "history" (Molina et al., 2018). Such a unique and complex intertwining of temporal dimensions provides everyday psychological experience with peculiar qualities that become the object of cultural psychology.

A successful attempt to include temporality as a methodological principle is represented by Sato's *Trajectory Equifinality Model* (Sato, Mori & Valsiner, 2016), which builds a "map" of the personal trajectory during the life course to understand how the person makes sense of her life choices in significant turning points and coordinates past–future tension.

DIALOGICALITY

A human being is never alone. The others are not only *around* us but also *inside* us as we internalize their voices that become parts of our psychological landscape. This is so strong and ubiquitous that many cultures developed specific practices in order to achieve momentary detachments from others. The famous actor and director Konstantin Stanislavski (1863–1938) recounted how he developed specific techniques after experiencing stage fright (Stanislavski, 1924). In order to exclude the influence of the audience and focus on the performance, he developed the concept of "public solitude", which the actor would achieve by using lights and prompts on the stage until becoming able to forget the presence of others around. Many Asian philosophies developed meditation practices to help with locking the world out and the others, at least temporarily. The need for using such devices signals the persistence of the *other-around* and the *other-in-mind* in the psychic life of human beings. Nevertheless, psychology does not always pay attention to the role of the others.

Ivana Marková (2016) distinguished between non-interactional and interactional epistemologies in psychology. Non-interactional epistemologies are those based on the subject–object independence as fundament of knowledge production. These are all the approaches in psychology that require distancing and exclusion of subjective biases as ways of constructing "objective" knowledge of the *world out there*. Interactional epistemologies are those that consider the production of knowledge as a whole situation, in which "subjects (e.g., knowers, individuals, elements, organisms) and objects that environ them (e.g. the known, contexts, Umwelt, environments) form irreducible ontological, that is, existential, units" (Marková, 2016, p. 91). Once the different agents enter a research situation, they become part of a whole and develop a common history (Tateo & Marsico, 2014). Cultural psychology is based on interactional epistemology and its methodology involves the principle of *dialogicality*: "The unbreakable existential unit underlying dialogicality comprises the Self and Other(s) (or the Ego–Alter). 'Others' could be other humans or human creations such as institutions, historically and culturally established traditions, morals, customs, and so on" (Marková, 2016, p. 93).

George Herbert Mead (1863–1931) was an American pragmatist philosopher, sociologist, and psychologist, He is regarded as one of the founders of symbolic interactionism, and one of founders of the Chicago School of Sociology

The principle of *dialogicality* derives from Vygotsky's concept of higher mental functions', sociogenesis – all mental processes are internalized social relationships (see Chapter 1); from Mead's interactionism (Mead, 1913) and from Bakhtin's concept of dialogism – all discourses imply more than one entity, the author, the narrator, the audience, and all the other texts produced in each culture. Every act of meaning-making is part of an ongoing dialogue between (real or imaginary) agents – each one with its own perspective and voice – who respond to each other. Every message is at the same time a message for the other and a message for me myself. In social interactions, the person engages in a "trialogue that involves one internal feed-forward loop that is coordinated with two social relations loops – ME < > ME and ME < > YOU" (Valsiner, 2018, p. 285). I see myself through the eyes of the others (internalized social other) and I see the others through myself (projected Self) (Figure 2.5).

Both the intra- and interpersonal dialogue work through the production and interpretation of signs (see Chapter 1). So, it is not based only on verbal messages. For instance, imagine waking up on the morning of an important job interview. You do not feel very self-confident and are afraid of performing poorly. You think you will fail and say to yourself "I am not worth it" (inner dialogue between Me and I). Then you remember that fashion brand watch your partner gave you and decide to wear it (the internalized voice of the other). As you wear the watch and look yourself in the mirror, you feel better and more confident. You feel like you are sending a message through

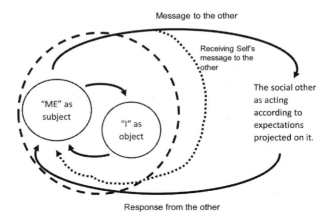

Figure 2.5 Me<>Other dialogical relationships

your outfit (interpersonal dialogue with projected social other). The watch becomes the sign through which the multiple voices establish a polyphonic dialogue between me and myself (signs operate on the self to regulate my inner psychic state); and of me with the social other (signs are used to externalize my psychic state, sending a message to the other). Finally, the anticipated response of the projected social other to my message (I expect the other to notice my watch) affects in return my psychic state (feel more confident).

The Dutch psychologist Hubert Hermans developed a systematic model of the polyphony of voices called *Dialogical Self Theory* (Hermans & Gieser, 2011). In summary, Dialogical Self Theory claims that the person develops a "society of self" with the internalized voices of significant others encountered during the life course (Hermans, 2001). The Self is a polyphonic synthesis of the internalized voices (called I-positions), e.g., the parents, the partner, the teacher, the friends, but also the media, etc., which voice a certain aspect of the self. When the person needs to make sense of something, the different voices provide the repertoires of meanings, values, idiosyncrasies that exist in the world outside. They are our personal version of our social experiences. The meaning-making process is a constant dialogue between the internalized I-positions that can result in conflict, agreement, alliance, between them. The history of the dialogue between those I-positions reflects both our personal development and our social trajectory. However, the continuous production and interpretation of meanings requires a work of organization over time. So, how do we build the sense of a stable Self while dealing with such a polyphony?

NARRATIVITY

So far, we have seen how the methodology to study psychological phenomena in cultural psychology must take into account temporality (in irreversible time) and polyphony (of internalized voices). What are the means by which human beings put together different voices along the flowing of time in between their personal experience and the collective life? Let's look at the following example:

> Now I shall tell everything. And I shall. Otherwise I should never venture forward to that page. It may also be necessary to do this for your sake, in the interests of orientation.
> Once I killed a man. His name was John Wakefield and I murdered him one night seventeen years ago in Misery Harbor.
> Many there were who became murderers in those days. The World War was raging, but that was legalized murder and meritorious slaughter. It was probably all one to the victims whether their murder had been legalized or not, but not so to the murderers.
> (Sandemose, 1936, p. 10)

This is the *incipit* of the novel *A fugitive crosses his tracks*, by the Norwegian writer Aksel Sandemose (1936). At the beginning of the novel, Sandemose introduces a narrator of a story (*I shall tell everything*) to an audience (*to do this for your sake*). The narrator also happens to be the main character of the story (*Once I killed a man*), but it could have been a different person. The story takes place in a space/time (*The World War was raging*). However, the time has more than one direction (*And I shall have to begin with the end*; *one night seventeen years ago*).

Now, take a second example:

> When Suleiman was killed, we had three children. The youngest was one and a half years old, and the oldest was five. My parents asked me if I wanted to come to them, and I said that I wanted to stay in my house. Two wives, we were like sisters, like friends. Her home was on the first floor, and when I came home from work, she would call me and give me food so that I could rest afterward. She is a quiet woman, not problematic.
> (Ben-Asher & Bokek-Cohen, 2019, p. 510)

The excerpt also talks about a killing. It is part of an interview with a widow of an Israeli soldier as part of a research by Ben-Asher and Bokek-Cohen on emotional labor among war widows (2019). In the second case, the narrator is telling a story involving many characters (Suleiman; herself; other widows; her parents). In this story there are also different temporalities (*When Suleiman was killed*; *She is a quiet woman*).

While the first example is the beginning of a fictional novel, the second is an excerpt from a real woman telling her life story during a research interview. Nevertheless, one can recognize some common aspects: they are both referring to an experience of killing in the form of storytelling. The reader can recognize and interpret the story in a certain way, so that similar meanings can be produced among different readers. Why is it so easy for people to recognize a story? And why do people tell stories?

Narrative and paradigmatic ways of thinking

The great psychologist Jerome Bruner (see Chapter 1) developed the idea that human beings have two complementary modalities of thinking when it comes to organizing their knowledge and their experiences in the world. He called the two modalities *paradigmatic thought* and *narrative thought* (Bruner, 1986), each with their own logic and rules. Paradigmatic thought, what is commonly considered logical thinking, is used when there is the need to categorize and classify, to establish causal and logical connections between things. A ranking, an alphabetical ordering or the classification of animal species are all examples of paradigmatic thinking. The narrative mode of thinking is used to represent reality analogically. Narrative is an organization of experience according to the rule of *verisimilitude* to real life, as-it-was in the past, as-it-is in the present, and as-if in the future. Besides, narrative thinking is about understanding and explaining the justifications for people's actions and about exploring possible alternatives.

> The term *then* functions differently in the logical proposition 'if x, then y' and in the narrative *recit* 'The king died, and then the queen died.' One leads to a search for universal truth conditions, the other for likely particular connections between two events – mortal grief, suicide, foul play.
>
> (Bruner, 1986, pp. 11–12)

In other words, we use narrative thinking when we need to make sense of our own and other life events beyond the pure visible facts. We tell stories because we want to make sense of what happened to us and to others, to explain why people acted in a certain way, but also to imagine different possible alternatives (Bruner, 1986; 2002). Narrative and paradigmatic modes of thinking are always present, and one continuously switches from one to the other when making sense of the world. Traditionally, paradigmatic thinking was associated with formal logic and hard sciences, in other words with non-interactionist epistemologies (Marková, 2016). Narrative mode of thought has been mainly associated with qualitative research (Clandinin, 2022), interactionist epistemologies, and common-sense thinking (Marková, 2016). However, they are both very important in research to the point that any data analysis can be considered as the construction of a narrative (Feigenbaum & Alamalhodaei, 2020).

Narrativity and sense-making

Narrativity seems to be a ubiquitous and universal feature of human beings. In every human collective there are ways of telling stories to make sense of the world. They may take the form of myths, legends, epics, fairy tales, novels, autobiographies, etc. They may follow different storytelling rules and different structures. They may sometimes violate the local cultural rules to invent amazing new forms of stories. However, one is often able to tell how a "good" story sounds, and good storytellers are praised and honored. When we are asked to talk about ourselves, we always present a narrative form, often modeling our autobiographical story on one of the models that circulate in our culture. Expressions such as "self-made man", "Cinderella complex", "Peter Pan complex", "Oedipus complex", "my life is a novel", "bohemian", etc. signal how we use archetypes and model stories in everyday life without even being aware of their origin. So, stories are told to imitate and account for real life, but our accounts and interpretations of what actually happened in real life imitate the stories we have learned. Moreover, narratives are the contexts in which one can play with possibilities and imagination (see Chapter 4), can try alternatives, and introduce innovations. Violation of the norm is one of the main ingredients of a "good" story.

Cultural psychology is interested in how people make sense of all their everyday experiences within the framework of their local culture. Everyday experiences may be mundane (as preparing food and raising children) or exceptional (as composing a symphony) but they involve all psychological functions and a synthesis between personal and collective meanings. Narratives can be very personal or collective – they can include persons, families, towns, nations, divinities, or even other worlds. Narrativity is the sovereign form of organizing experience and needs to be included in every methodological effort. The *content* of a narrative is important as much as the *way* the story is told.

What type of knowledge can we produce about the way people make meaning through a narrative mode of thinking, or what are the functions of narrativity?

- *Positioning*: every story implies a narrator and some characters. The narrator can take different positions in relation to the characters. The narrator can coincide with the protagonist of the story (*I am talking about myself*) or can take a different position (*I am talking about that guy X*). The narrator can tell a story in the first person singular (as "I") or plural (as "we"). All the different positions imply a different configuration of relations (obligations, duties, rights, belonging, distancing, etc.) between the actors (Harré, 2012).
- *Perspective taking*: the choice of a position implies a particular perspective. This requires the effort of putting oneself "in the shoes" of another.

For instance, the Polish writer Andrej Zaniewski (1994) wrote the incredible autobiography of a rat during World War II. His extreme effort in perspective taking provided a distancing that allowed him to see how human beings behave in the terrible times of war. However, when one takes the perspective of the other, one brings one's own luggage of assumptions, prejudices, and beliefs, turning the process into a dialogue between multiple positions (Guimaraes, 2011).

- *Diachronicity*: a narrative is an account of events occurring over time(s). It is irreducibly durative (Bruner, 1991), and can play on different levels of temporality (see above). Irreversible time is an inescapable existential fact, but storytelling allows temporality to be played with at the symbolic level so that one can reverse, zoom in and out, overlap time, like in the first excerpt above (Sandemose, 1936).
- *Contextualization*: narratives are about happenings in a specific time/space, but they go from the particular to the abstract. A particular character or event "achieves its emblematic status by its embeddedness in a story that is in some sense generic" (Bruner, 1991, p. 7). This is how, for instance, the story of two particular adolescents such as Romeo and Juliet can become the emblematic and universal model of unfortunate love.
- *Intentionality*: "Narratives are about people acting in setting, and the happenings that befall them must be relevant to their intentional states while so engaged to their beliefs, desires, theories, values, and so on" (Bruner, 1991, p. 7). Through the stories one tries to understand agency but also its limitations. Stories make sense about *why* people acted but also which *intervening* factors affected their agency (helping or disrupting their plans).
- *Modal thinking*: stories are not mere accounts of "happenings" or "facts". The stories are arenas of modal thinking, that is opportunities to talk about how things could, must, or could not have been. Modal thinking, involving an imaginative work (see Chapter 4) is at the same time a way of sanctioning undesired behaviors (Pandora punished for her curiosity); and to open new possible worlds and developmental trajectories (utopian tales) (Bruner, 1991; Valsiner, 2009).
- *Violation of canonicity*: modal thinking is strictly related to the tension between prescribed scripts and unexpected ruptures. Narratives require scripts as context, but they are not sufficient for narrativity (Bruner, 1991). A "good" story implies some breach of an implicit canonical script and some turning points, even if only to find a way to restore the canonicity. People tend to narrate their autobiographies in terms of ruptures and reparations in relation to an implicit canonical script (Zittoun et al., 2003). Moreover, the relevance of violation relies in its potentiality to resist the reparation of canonicity and to open new unexpected possibilities (Bruner, 1991).
- *Justifying*: narratives are constructed to make sense of people actions. If someone (including oneself) is acting in a certain way, there *must*

be a reason. This need to make sense is so strong that many narrative forms – such as myths, legends, and sacred texts – construct stories in which objects, abstract concepts, or natural forces are anthropomorphized in order to find reasons for their "actions" (Tateo, 2018).

- *Customizability*: the term comprises two different aspects. First, narratives are *customary*. They involve normativity, ethos, habits, good and ritual ways of doing: "A breach presupposes a norm" (Bruner, 1991, p. 15). But narratives are also flexible and adaptable, they can be combined and recombined, can be accrued, or summarized. In other words, narratives are also *customable*. Narratives are temporal configurations of whole/parts relationships – that is, they are ecosystems of meaning. They can be adapted to specific socio-historical or personal situations and can be *translated* from one context to another.

Narrativity is not of course a feature only of stories in verbal form. Every complex of signs can have the attribute of narrativity. The sacred themes in visual arts are a very good example of how particular events can be generalized to promote desired behavior and inhibit undesired outcomes (Figure 2.6).

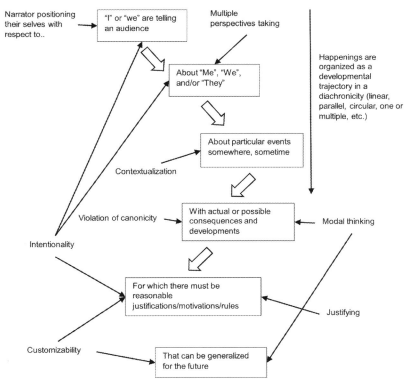

Figure 2.6 Features of narrativity

THE FORMS OF KNOWING

Figure 2.7 Engraving by Albrecht Dürer (1504) showing Adam and Eve in the Garden of Eden (https://commons.wikimedia.org/wiki/File:Albrecht_D%C3%BCrer,_Adam_and_Eve,_1504,_Engraving.jpg)

In the engraving by Albrecht Dürer, Adam and Eve are represented in the Garden of Eden just before the Snake is passing the forbidden fruit of knowledge to Eve (Figure 2.7). The artist is positioning himself as spectator and narrator, telling an audience the story of two particular individuals, Adam and Eve, which happened in a given space/time. The characters violate canonicity by intentionally breaking God's rule. The justification is the persuasive power of the Devil/Snake, which is nevertheless not sufficient to absolve them from their sin against God. The particular developmental event and its consequences become an abstract, transferable, and generalizable sign of the danger of breaking God's rules and of the value of knowledge, which will promote or inhibit further actions in the future by the audience.

From this overview, it appears how narrativity plays a very important role in everyday meaning-making, sewing together the threads of time, the polyphony of voices and the personal belonging to a larger cultural collective. It becomes particularly important in the case of *autobiographical* and

Key concept

Methodology is the process of goal-oriented thinking and interventional procedures used by the investigator in interaction with the investigated phenomena, which leads to the construction of new knowledge.

testimonial narratives (Bruner, 2002). Thus, together with temporality and dialogicality, it is part of the methodology in cultural psychology.

QUALITATIVE METHODS TO STUDY DEVELOPING LIVING SYSTEMS

Now that we have become acquainted with the main principles of the epistemology of cultural psychology, we can outline the characteristics of methodology in cultural psychology. Usually, university students are introduced very early to the method's dualism (quantitative *versus* qualitative) as there were two opposite *parties*. They are required to make a choice between the *objective* and *scientific* way of measurement and the dark side of *subjective* and *anecdotal* knowledge. However, the object of psychology is the personal experience unfolding within a network of (socio-material–cultural) agents. Quantitative methods translate the quality of the psychic experience into numbers, while qualitative methods translate the quality of psychic experience into (mainly) verbal accounts. *Both* numbers and verbal accounts are types of signs representing *qualities* of psychic phenomena. Measurable dimensions (quantities) are just one of the qualities that the researcher can over-impose on psychic phenomena. This is a social construction deriving from the dominant status attributed in neoliberal societies to specific types of symbols (numbers) and artifacts (technological apparatuses), which are considered more *real* and *objective* than other symbols, such as words or images. This dualism represents a superficial opposition. Besides the type of signs used to represent them, the object of psychology concerns the qualities of psychic phenomena. Thus, methodology of psychology must be able to grasp qualitative developments of living systems, and quantitative methods are a specific sub-category that translates such qualities into numbers and figures, giving the impression that qualities can be expressed more objectively through the magnitude of fragmented analytical variables. Such a confusion is possible because the relationship between methodology and methods is not always fully articulated.

The methodological cycle

To present the methodological perspective of cultural psychology, we will thus begin from what Branco and Valsiner (1997) called the *methodological cycle* (Figure 2.8).

The methodology is a conceptual/empirical system of elements able to organize the relationship between the researcher as epistemic agent (who aims at producing knowledge); the system of meta-codes (shared general assumptions on the reality); the phenomenon (what one wants to understand or gain knowledge of); the theory constructed to understand (how one thinks the phenomenon can work); and the methods constructed to answer the curiosity (how one can observe the phenomenon and make some of its features visible). The

Key concept

Methods are techniques that are applied to solve a problem, like obtaining *data*, depending upon current fashions in the discipline or the perceived validity value.

Methods without the system are meaningless.

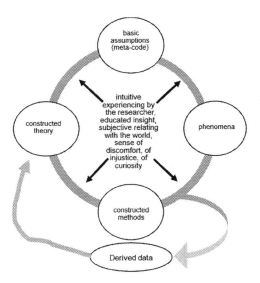

Figure 2.8 The methodological cycle (Branco & Valsiner, 1997)

data are thus not a real specimen of the phenomenon, rather a constructed representation of its parts that the researcher wants to make visible. For instance, if the researcher is "measuring" the magnitude of a construct (e.g., "anxiety"), it does not imply that the conventional representation on a 10-point scale of a variable corresponds to the real quality of the psychic experience.

According to Branco and Valsiner (1997), the methodological system is a *cycle* because it entails a recursive process. In the conventional methodological teaching, the primacy is attributed to the direction theory>methods>phenomenon. Starting from a theoretical framework, applying the correct methods, the researcher can verify the hypothesis on the nature of the phenomenon. However, this is a partial understanding of the cycle. One can start from any of the points to understand how the theory is always based on some general assumptions (for instance, on the nature of the human mind and its relation to the brain) that also privilege a class of phenomena. What is usually neglected, but is extremely relevant in cultural psychology, is the role of the investigator who is the very first instrument of the research. As cultural psychology is interested in deeply human phenomena, the researcher's educated intuition becomes a powerful epistemic instrument to identify potentially relevant phenomena or critically deconstruct the (often implicit) meta-assumptions of theory.

The focus of cultural psychology is developmental. Any method we create and use (qualitative, quantitative, mixed) must be able to account for the principles of temporality, dialogicality, and narrativity.

A large part of qualitative research is based on verbal accounts (interviews, diaries, etc.) or in the numerical representation of verbal accounts (questionnaires, scales, etc.). Language is of course the main form of organizing

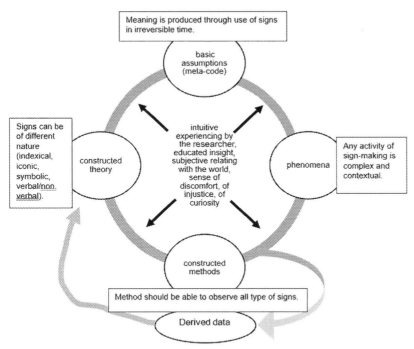

Figure 2.9 The methodological cycle in the semiotic perspective

psychic life but not the only one. Some psychic events are "below" or "above" the threshold of verbal language. To overcome this restriction, we need to design a methodological cycle that incorporates semiosis as the form of living systems. Figure 2.9 shows the methodological cycle once we replace the traditional verbal/non verbal distinction in psychology with the concept of sign, which can be produced and interpreted in different modalities.

The starting point of our methodological perspective is found in the educated insight of the researcher. Mainstream methods training recommends silencing the researcher's subjectivity as source of bias. In our perspective instead, meaningful research questions emerge from the subjective experiencing of a sense of something "out of place", that can be triggered by intellectual curiosity, by sense of unfairness and injustice, or by intimate experiences. The meta-code assumptions involve meaning-making as a semiotic process that unfolds in irreversible time – that is any activity of sign production and interpretation is a legitimate object of interest for cultural psychology, from mundane everyday small talk to the products of artistic invention, from communication between human and non-human living beings to the laboratory research situation itself. The principles of temporality, dialogicality, and narrativity inform the construction of theories and methods. Cultural psychology has no fetishism of the method. Methods alone are meaningless if they are not part of a methodological system. The construction of methods must follow the qualitative nature of psychic phenomena. In the next chapters, we will explore some of those phenomena and concepts that have been studied in cultural psychology.

SUMMARY OF CHAPTER 2

In this chapter, we have presented the epistemic principles that inform the methodology of cultural psychology. First, the fundamental focus on the different levels of temporality. We started from the concept of irreversible time that provides psychic experience with the existential features of uniqueness. Then, we discussed the principle of temporality. All psychic events take place in spatio/temporal coordinates. This makes phenomena contextual, historical, and requires the understanding of their genesis and development. Temporality is articulated in several coexisting dimensions, whose interaction contributes to the production of meaning.

The second principle is dialogicality: meaning-making is produced between respons(able) agents. The production of meaning is the result of a dialogue between different perspectives, internalized and externalized. The principle of narrativity shows how meaning is organized in the intersection between personal and concrete levels with abstract, generalizable, and custom(ized) forms of narrative.

Finally, we have discussed the methodological cycle in cultural psychology, showing the relations between the different elements of the system to produce new knowledge. The methodological cycle organizes the different parts of the research situation and articulates the concepts of semiosis, irreversible time, temporality, dialogicality, and narrativity to help define the empirical ways to make the phenomenon of study visible. The researcher is an integral part of the cycle and their subjective educated insight is very valuable in research.

Check your knowledge and reflect

Task: Try to imagine how to study an everyday activity that you can observe (e.g., watching a concert, using public transport, doing sport, going to church, etc.; you can also choose the same topic as in Chapter 1) and try to imagine how to study it. Identify the elements of the methodological cycle in your study (phenomenon, theory, methods, etc.) and use your educated intuition to find an original and innovative way to observe the phenomenon. It is important your methodology can capture the temporal, dialogical, and narrative aspects. Write a short essay (maximum two pages; you can include images that you take) elaborating your personal view and using the concepts presented so far. Then, share your essay with two colleagues and ask for their feedback.

NOTE

1 This insight is developed by Jaan Valsiner in several of his works.

REFERENCES

Bakhtin, M. (1981). Forms of time and of the chronotope in the novel. In M. Bakhtin (Ed.), *The dialogic imagination* (pp. 84–258). Austin, TX: University of Texas Press.

Bastos, A. C. S., Valsiner, J., & Uriko, K. (Eds.). (2012). *Cultural dynamics of women's lives*. Charlotte, NC: IAP.

Ben-Asher, S., & Bokek-Cohen, Y. (2019). Liminality and emotional labor among war widows in Israel. *Culture & Psychology*, 25(4), 503–516.

Branco, A. U., & Valsiner, J. (1997). Changing methodologies: A co-constructivist study of goal orientations in social interactions. *Psychology and Developing Societies*, 9(1), 35–64.

Bruner, J. S. (1986). *Actual minds, possible worlds*. Cambridge, MA: Harvard University Press.

Bruner, J. (1991). The narrative construction of reality. *Critical Inquiry*, 18(1), 1–21.

Bruner, J. S. (2002). *Making stories: Law, literature, life*. New York: Farrar, Straus & Giroux.

Chakrabarty, D. (2021). *The climate of history in a planetary age*. Chicago, IL: University of Chicago Press.

Clandinin, D. J. (2022). *Engaging in narrative inquiry*. London: Routledge.

Driesch, H. (1925). *The crisis in psychology*. Princeton, NJ: Princeton University Press.

Feigenbaum, A., & Alamalhodaei, A. (2020). *The data storytelling workbook*. London: Routledge.

Guimaraes, D. S. (2011). Amerindian anthropology and cultural psychology: Crossing boundaries and meeting otherness' worlds. *Culture & Psychology*, 17(2), 139–157.

Harré, R. (2012). Positioning theory: Moral dimensions of social-cultural psychology. In J. Valsiner (Ed.), *Oxford handbook of culture and psychology* (pp. 191–206). Oxford: Oxford University Press.

Hermans, H. (2001). The dialogical self: Toward a theory of personal and cultural positioning. *Culture and Psychology*, 7(3), 243–281.

Hermans, H., & Gieser, T. (Eds.). (2011). *Handbook of dialogical self theory*. Cambridge: Cambridge University Press. https://doi.com/10.1017/CBO9781139030434

Kant, I. (1896). *Immanuel Kant's critique of pure reason*. New York: Macmillan.

Lehmann, O. V. (2016). Silence and sense-making. In S. H. Klempe (Ed.), *Cultural psychology of musical experiences* (pp. 281–298). Charlotte, NC: IAP.

Marková, I. (2016) *The dialogical mind*. Boston, MA: Cambridge University Press.

Mead, G. H. (1913). The social self. *Journal of Philosophy, Psychology and Scientific Methods*, 10(14), 374–380.

Molina, M. E., et al. (2018). Temporality as the co-construction of couple relationship: The regulation of experiential time. *Culture & Psychology*, 24(4), 512–528. https://doi.com/10.1177/1354067x17737719

Russon, J. (1998). Reading Hegel's phenomenology. Bloomington and Indianapolis, IN: Indiana University Press.

Sandemose, A. (1936). *A fugitive crosses his tracks*. Translated by E. Gay-Tifft. New York: A. A. Knopf.

Sato, T., Mori, N., & Valsiner, J. (Eds.). (2016). *Making of the future: The trajectory equifinality approach in cultural psychology*. Charlotte, NC: IAP.

Simão, L. M., Guimarães, D. S., & Valsiner, J. (Eds.). (2015). *Temporality: Culture in the flow of human experience*. Charlotte, NC: IAP.

Stanislavski, K. (1924). *My life in art*. Translated by J. J. Robbins. Boston, MA: Little & Brown.

Tateo, L. (2018). Nature unveiling herself before science. In G. Jovanović, L. Allolio-Näcke, & C. Ratner (Eds.), *The challenges of cultural psychology: Historical legacies and future responsibilities* (pp. 59–74). London: Routledge.

Tateo, L., & Marsico, G. (2014). Open complementarity in cultural psychology. In B. Wagoner, N. Chaudhary, & P. Hviid (Eds.), *Cultural psychology and its future: Complementarity in a new key* (pp. 77–91). Charlotte, NC: IAP.

Tateo, L., & Valsiner, J. (2015). Time breath of psychological theories: A meta-theoretical focus. *Review of General Psychology, 19*(3), 357–364. https://doi.org/10.1037/gpr0000035

Tisdall, K., Davis, J., Fry, D., Konstantoni, K., Kustatscher, M., Maternowska, C., & Weiner, L. (2023). *Critical childhood studies: Global perspectives.* London: Bloomsbury.

Valsiner, J. (2009). Between fiction and reality: Transforming the semiotic object. *Σημειωτκή-Sign Systems Studies, 37*(1–2), 99–113.

Valsiner, J. (2014). *An invitation to cultural psychology.* London: Sage. https://doi.org/10.4135/9781473905986

Valsiner, J. (2017). *From methodology to methods in human psychology.* Cham: Springer. https://doi.org/10.1007/978-3-319-61064-1

Valsiner, J. (2018). Culture within development: Similarities behind differences. In G. Marsico & J. Valsiner (Eds.), *Beyond the mind: Cultural dynamics of the psyche* (pp. 271–292). Charlotte, NC: Information Age Publishing.

Zaniewski, A. (1994). *Rat: A novel.* New York: Arcade Publishing.

Zittoun, T., Duveen, G., Gillespie, A., Ivinson, G., & Psaltis, C. (2003). The use of symbolic resources in developmental transitions. *Culture & Psychology, 9*(4), 415–448.

Zittoun, T., Valsiner, J., Salgado, J., Vedeler, D., Gonçalves, M. M., & Ferring, D. (2013). *Human development in the life course: Melodies of living.* New York: Cambridge University Press.

CHAPTER 3

What is cultural psychology?

Scan the QR-code to access additional materials and watch outstanding international scholars discussing key concepts.

LEARNING GOALS

1. To critically reflect upon the common definitions of culture
2. To understand what is cultural psychology
3. To understand the concept of personal culture
4. To understand the limitations of current non-cultural or cross-cultural psychology

CHAPTER OVERVIEW

In this chapter, we discuss the concept of culture and its relationship with the mind. We will discuss the history of cultural psychology, the concept of personal culture, and the concept of window of acceptable possibilities. This will be followed by a discussion about the transition between cultures and the concept of proculturation. Finally, the difference between cultural psychology and cross-cultural psychology; the decolonization of psychology; and the ecology of mind and culture will be presented.

GROUP ACTIVITY FOR INSTRUCTOR: WHAT IS YOUR CULTURE?

The instructor asks the students to answer the question "What is your culture?". Based on their answers, the instructor will continue by asking "If you say that your culture is X, can you also say that there is a Y culture that is different from X?". For example, if a student answers, "My culture is French (or Italian, or academic, or Goth, etc.)", the instructor can ask: "What part of France are you from?" The student can answer "I am from Paris". Then, the instructor asks, "Would you say that there is a Paris culture that is different from French culture? Why?" The student will answer positively. The instructor continues by asking "Which part of Paris are you from?", "Is there a X culture that is different from Paris culture?", "Do you have a family culture that is different from the culture Y?", and so on. The discussion can continue until most of the students have contributed.

Reflection questions

The purpose of the activity is to observe many possible ways of delimiting culture and how people can identify with different, partially overlapping cultures. Possible questions for stimulating reflection are:

- How do you identify the characteristic of a culture?
- How many people do you need to have a culture?
- If there are so many possible cultures, how can this concept be useful to understand people?

CULTURE AS CULTIVATION: THE NORWEGIAN HOUSE

What does a typical Norwegian house look like? This was a very important question from the mid-19th century to the 1920s in Norway (Aas Solbakken et al., 2024). During that historical period, most European countries, including Norway, were indeed occupied with the construction of an independent national identity by the (more or less) imaginary production of a historical continuity to justify the project (Anderson, 1991). The problem of the origin, the roots, was extremely important to legitimate nationalist claims. Starting from the German Romantic period (late 18th–early 19th century; Adescola, 2013), everybody tried to build their own "imagined community" (Anderson, 1991). "Throughout the nineteenth century, Norwegian historians strove to connect the present with the historic 'Saga Age' (*c.*800–1300)" (Aas Solbakken et al., 2024, p. 135). But how do you give a body to an abstract concept such as "Norwegianness"? The solution of Norwegian architects was quite simple: first, you use the most local construction material: timber. Logs became the mark of the typical Norwegian building style, the strong encouragement from the important national timber industry (Aas Solbakken et al., 2024). The second invention of the Norwegian tradition was the so-called "dragestil" (dragon style) (Figure 3.1).

Architects and art historians rapidly codified the features of the typical Norwegian national architecture rooted in the rural tradition of churches, farms, and country houses. In particular, the so-called stave church, a type of rural church built with timber logs, was designed to be the architectural model (Figure 3.2b).

Figure 3.1 The dragon shape invented by the architect Holme Hansen Muthe (1848–98) (photo by Luca Tateo, 2024)

Figure 3.2 The two churches on opposite sides of the Norwegian Russian border in old images at the Oslo National Museum (photo by Luca Tateo, 2024)

It was relevant that the dragon style and the stave church were basically inventions and contemporary reinterpretation of what the intellectuals believed was a traditional architecture. What is relevant here is that the construction of a national identity is a process that involves both imaginative and non-imaginative (see Chapter 4) processes. It is based on some local conditions, such as the extensive availability of forests and the presence of an ancient Viking history, serving a future project of nation building. Culture is a process of cultivation. A Norwegian style building can even become a guard of national boundaries.

"One of Norway's most remarkable Dragestil churches is the Neiden Chapel in the High Artic region of Sør-Varanger, Finmark, consecrated in 1902" (Aas Solbakken et al., 2024, p. 138). The chapel (Figure 3.2b) is remarkable because of its counterpart, the large Orthodox Church in "typical" Russian style built on the other side of the Russian border (Figure 3.2a). Just like culture, artifacts are also cultivated (see Chapter 1). The region was at that time a Sami-populated area at the border between Norway and what is now Finland, but at that time was still part of the Russian empire. In 1874, the Russians expanded the old St. George chapel in the village of Boris Gelb into a larger orthodox church. "From a Norwegian perspective of the time, the demographical trends in Neiden were also worrisome, as the inhabitants were Skolt Sami and Kvens, with the only Norwegian resident being the family of the local teacher" (Aas Solbakken et al., 2024, p. 138). As a result, the two churches in the "typical" Russian (Figure 3.2a) and Norwegian (Figure 3.2b) styles respectively were sitting face to face on opposite sides of the border, which was marked by a river and united by two parts of a village. This example clearly shows the role of signs in cultural cultivation. The border conflict and the ethnic expansion was indeed masked by religious proselytism. The churches built in a (partially imaginary) traditional national style became signs of the active presence of a certain cultural community. Before being a conflict between land borders, the struggle was to conquer souls and minds through the dissemination of signs of "Norwegianness" and "Russianness" (for whatever that means, as we have seen in the initial activity) in the environment. As the cultivation of certain types of plants in the environment contributes to promoting a cultural identity, so does the cultivation of artifacts such as buildings. One can find examples in the "typical" landscapes of some regions, like the tulip fields and windmills in the Netherlands; the grass fields and flocks of sheep in Great Britain; the vineyards in Italy; the rice fields in Vietnam; or the tea plantations in India, etc. Culture is *naturalized* through *artificial* cultivation of environmental signs that constantly mark the presence of a shared and stable identity.

DO WE NEED CULTURE?

This is a book about "cultural psychology" thus, there must be some type of relationship between "culture" and "psychology", whilst at the same time, one cannot be completely reduced to the other. It is well known that hundreds of different definitions of "culture" exist in the social and human sciences (Descola, 2013; Kroeber & Kluckhohn, 1952; Vermeersch, 1978). The first distinction is whether "culture" can be considered a specific attribute of the human species or if non-human species also have some type of culture. Of course, this delimitation depends on how we define culture and what are the minimal requirements for identifying it (e.g., use of artifacts; non-genetic intergenerational transmission; language; organized social life; etc.), and it has changed over the centuries. This sounds a circular argument: culture is a human peculiarity to the extent that we do not consider non-human phenomena as "cultural". The "humanistic" conception of culture (Descola, 2013, p. 72) equates it with "civilization" and led to the typical colonialist attitude of dismissing all phenomena that did not comply with the European standards as "primitive" and "uncivilized". When European colonizers entered into contact with indigenous populations in South America or Australia, those cultures were not recognized as human cultures to the extent that their products were not acknowledged as cultural artifacts (Ciofalo, 2019). For instance, James Cook reported in his journal that aboriginals were the first people without religion, and that they had no civilization, as they were showing no sign of crop cultivation or "typical" rituals apparently (Williams, 2023).

Anthropology proposed a "culturalist" approach to the problem (Boas, 1904); that is, there are as many "cultures" as human collectives and all have their own richness and peculiarity (Descola, 2013). However, in this case, there is the problem of defining the *borders* of a culture (see Chapter 5). How far back in time, how many people must be involved, how different from other "cultures" for a phenomenon to be called a culture? For instance, the "main" cultures have major stable patterns of ways of doing, talking, believing, eating, etc. Within larger cultures, one can identify smaller and situated patterns, so-called sub-cultures, with a shorter temporal duration and a smaller number of members (e.g., pop culture, punk culture, gaming culture, etc.).

Nevertheless, the underlying idea of culture that is implicit in most of social sciences and informs cross-cultural approaches was developed during the German Romantic period in the 19th century. It embodies the idea that when people are born in the same land from a lineage of generations and share the same language, they are like-minded. It is the German concept of the *Volk*: people who belong to the same culture (read *nation*) share the "*Volkgeist* (spirit of the people) of Herder, the *Nationalcharakter* (of Wilhelm von Humboldt, and the *Völkergedanken* (folk ideas) of Bastian" (Descola, 2013, p. 74). This concept is so powerful that even today cross-cultural studies assume that nationality overlaps with culture. Moreover, school systems are based on the idea of a dominant national language, so that migrant students can be included only if they accept being culturally assimilated.

Franz Uri Boas was one of the initiators of the movement that moved away from the positivistic idea of comparing cultures—to assess their development, measured on the reference scale of Western societies—to the postmodernist idea of the cross-cultural, that is, the idea that culture can be treated as an independent variable that influences psycho-social processes, otherwise universals.

Franz Uri Boas (1858–1942) was a German-American pioneer of modern anthropology. He initiated historical particularism and cultural relativism in opposition to scientific racism.

> In psychological anthropology the important questions are the discovery of a system of the evolution of culture, the study of the modifications of simple general traits under the influence of different geographical and social conditions, the question of transmission and spontaneous origin, and that of folk psychology versus individual psychology.
>
> (Boas, 1904, p. 521)

In the former case, the voicing of the "other" culture is almost silenced by the dominant one. In the latter case, the cross-cultural approach is unidirectional. Indeed, one can hardly find cross-cultural studies that do not assume as baseline the perspective of the dominant culture. Thus, cross-cultural studies imply a comparison of some psycho-social dimensions of the Western culture, namely the Anglo-Saxon culture, with the "others", rather than the other way round. Seldom can one read a cross-cultural study between populations of the United States and any African country from the point of view of the indigenous psychology.

Besides, the idea of "cross-cultural" is based on two main assumptions:

a) the universality of psycho-social processes, that is a kind of "human nature" or "natural brain" which is shared by all different civilizations;
b) the assumption that a shared culture *must* produce shared behaviors (Valsiner, 2014).

These two assumptions lead to the paradox of believing in both the homogeneity and heterogeneity of cultures at the same time (Valsiner, 2014). On the one hand, cultures must be internally homogeneous because of the binding force and the capability of culture to shape behavior. Homogeneity must also be present between cultures, to the extent that they are based on some latent universal features of human nature, independently of the specific contextual conditions, albeit these features can differ in quantity (e.g., individualism/collectivism). On the other hand, cultures must be heterogeneous in their diversity, because otherwise no comparison would be possible.

Cultural psychology is in a certain sense the main opponent of the idea of culture as a reified entity that can guide individual life. First, culture does not exist outside, or despite of, the person. Second, when we treat culture as an *explanans*, like in cross-cultural studies, we need first to circumscribe the culture we are talking about. What is the level of analysis one should focus on? Culture is clearly not homogeneous. The reification of cultures as a sort of container and content can be called a *sarcophagus model of culture* (Figure 3.3). Understanding culture as a mere container or naturalizing it as a territory produces a nested system of sub-cultures and sub-sub-cultures, of overlapping classifications that are fuzzy and sometimes misleading. For instance, one assumes that standard variables such as gender

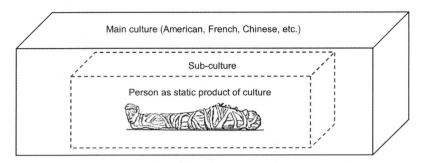

Figure 3.3 The sarcophagus model of cultural comparison

or age are important in defining sub-cultures, rather than *proving* that they are. Opening one layer of the sarcophagus after another, the person as active cultural agent is overlooked.

The personal psyche "belongs" or is "determined" by a static and internally homogeneous culture. At the end, the individual psyche becomes an unanimated *mummy*, a mummified entity without temporality and life, instead of the active agent who produces, uses, and elaborates culture.

So, if there are hundreds of different definitions of culture (Kroeber & Kluckhohn, 1952; Vermeersch, 1978), if culture is not a container, a place to which people passively "belong" or are "influenced" by (Valsiner, 2014), if culture is not an "independent variable" that can explain people's behavior (Valsiner, 2014), do we still need "culture" as heuristic concept in cultural psychology? Indeed, hegemonic North American psychology tried either to get rid of culture to explain mental life and to establish a universalistic view of psychic processes based on the common biological features of human beings, or to reduce culture to a simple set of measurable behavioral indicators.

On the other hand, the concept of culture has been constructed by modernity in opposition to nature (Descola, 2013). This dualism has led to the difficult and controversial scientific project of defining which part of human "essence" belonged to nature and which to culture. Following a hierarchy that originated with Aristotle, those human features that were closer to the natural state made humans part of the animal realm (so called-lower mental functions). The features that were typical of culture constituted the higher mental functions (i.e., logic, language, etc.) that made humans superior to the rest of living species. Hence, recognizing or not higher mental functions in some categories of people (children, women, disabled, etc.) or some cultures (indigenous cultures) was a way to attribute value (see the discussion on decolonization in the next pages).

The cultural–developmental perspective in psychology has overcome this sterile dualism by conceptualizing the "triple helix" (Lewontin, 2000) of human development, where bio-cultural-historical dimensions feed into each other, creating a developmental niche for the ontogenetic and socio-genetic psychological development of the person (Cole & Packer, 2016). In summary, a person cannot be reduced to the outcome of either her biological or cultural influences. The person is rather a unique synthesis of the historical relationship between the organism and the environment, which are *inclusively separated* (see Chapter 1).

According to cultural psychology, culture is not a variable, it has no agency, whereas people have (Valsiner, 2014). One cannot use culture as a cause to explain and generalize human behavior. Culture can be considered a frame, a system of meanings, practices, and artifacts that is ill-defined and fuzzy to the extent that it is always constructed, re-constructed and demolished by people's actions. The system of signs, meanings, and practices is collective, internalized by the person during their lifetime. Yet persons produce unique versions of personal cultures, their personally idiosyncratic semiotic system of symbols, practices, and objects whose creation is oriented and channeled by the collective tradition, its suggestions, and demands (Valsiner, 2014).

FIRST, SECOND, AND THIRD NATURE

Another useful approach to the understanding of the relationship between cultural and non-cultural dimensions of human psyche in relation to the environment has been proposed by Kalevi Kull (1998). In the case of human beings, the environment that affects (selectively perceived by the sense organs) and is affected (selectively modified through action) by the living organism (called *Umwelt*, see Chapter 4) is experienced semiotically (see Chapter 1).

> As a result of the differences humans can make, the nature in their Umwelt is distinguished into first, second, and third nature; what we think is outside the Umwelt, can be called zero nature. **Zero** nature is nature itself (e.g., absolute wilderness). **First** nature is the nature as we see, identify, describe and interpret it. **Second** nature is the nature which we have materially interpreted, this is materially translated nature, i.e. a changed nature, a produced nature. **Third** nature is a virtual nature, as it exists in art and science.
>
> (Kull, 1998, p. 355, emphasis in original)

One can see here how there is no discontinuity or dichotomy between "nature" and "culture". On the contrary, they mutually feed into each other. Indeed, the way human beings selectively perceive and recognize the elements in the environment are culturally mediated. One recognizes plants and animals and *gives names* to them. Those names can come from a shared cultural tradition (e.g., the flower *Narcissus* named after a Greek myth). Starting from those perceptual distinctions, human beings create a *second* nature, the so-called anthropic environment. "The building of second nature generally means that people apply certain models, or we may even say, certain

Figure 3.4 *Allegory of the Five Senses*, 1668, by Gérard de Lairesse, Kelvingrove Art Gallery and Museum, Glasgow. Public domain image (https://commons.wikimedia.org/wiki/File:1668_G%C3%A9rard_de_Lairesse_-_Allegory_of_the_Five_Senses.jpg)

general linguistic patterns upon nature" (Kull, 1998, p. 356). Landscapes are filled with human signs, artifacts, urban spaces are organized semiotically (Tateo & Marsico, 2023). Finally, the relationship with the environment is characterized by a *third nature*, that is a system of meanings which is totally symbolic (Figure 3.4) yet able to shape the person's interaction with the environment by, for instance, producing ideal and abstract models of "beauty", "rationality", etc.

In the allegorical Baroque painting, the human senses are represented as two women and three children engaged in some activities with their relative attributes. For instance, hearing is associated with the child playing music on a triangle. Sight holds a mirror on the floor. The woman representing taste has some fruit. The girl representing smell holds flowers. Finally, the woman representing touch has a bird perching on her raised hand. Allegories are pictorial descriptions of abstract concepts that guide the experience in a particular culture through *aesthetic suggestions to feel* in a particular way (Tateo, 2018). So, although the *third nature* is completely abstract and symbolic, it affects the *first nature* that is the way human beings perceive and act on the environment. Kull's (1998) model is a description in semiotic terms of how cultural features emerge from the organism's relationship with the environment, and how both the environment and the human organism itself (e.g., our senses) cannot be experienced other than in cultural terms.

Once we have understood that culture is neither a thing nor a container, we can start discussing how it could be useful to keep this concept and use it in relation to psychic life. This is exactly the purpose of cultural psychology and its way of understanding the mind–culture relationship. So, it is time to attempt a definition.

CULTURAL PSYCHOLOGY

Cultural psychology is the study of *third-level psychological processes*, such as meaning-making, imagining, constructive remembering (Wagoner, Brescó & Awad, 2019), affectivating (Cornejo et al., 2018), bordering (see Chapter 5), and teaching/learning. Third-level psychological processes are those complex personal and collectively coordinated human experiences that presuppose the hierarchical and dynamic integration of lower level (perception, attention, etc.) and higher-level mental functions (language, memory, reflection, etc.). Third-level psychological processes cannot be reduced to lower levels nor can they be considered in terms of single separated functions (e.g. cognition as separated from emotion). They constitute a systemic organization, in which whole–parts hierarchical integration makes the process possible. Cultural psychology does not have a single "object" of study. It rather studies relationships. Indeed, psychological experiences do not present as "things in themselves" but as relations of interaction between organisms and their surroundings. The *permanence and cultivation, collectively coordinated* of those relationships constitutes the "cultural" in cultural psychology.

Cultural psychology is not a discipline but a way of understanding psychological knowledge with a long story dating back to the early 16th century (Cole, 2003; Klempe, 2021; Tateo, 2015). The label covers a range of theoretical and empirical approaches to the study of the relationship between meaning, mind, and human activities in different cultural–historical contexts. Since the 1980s, the approaches of psychology interested in the use of the term "culture" flourished in the dialogue with different disciplines – such as anthropology, ethnography, history, philosophy, epigenetics, ecology, human geography, theology, cultural studies, etc. – and in the developmental processes of the organism in its historicity and context (Valsiner, 2019).

The different approaches to cultural psychology (Boesch, 1991; Bruner, 1990; Cole, 2003; Shweder, 1991; Wertsch, del Río & Alvarez, 1995; Valsiner, 2014) share the fundamental principle that the concept of culture is needed to understand the human mind. The common principles shared by cultural psychology's approaches are:

- *the centrality of the meaning-making processes*: meaning is a central existential and pragmatic category of human psyche. For humans everything *must have a meaning* to the point that we immediately look for motives, justifications, explanations for our own conduct and that of other humans – as well as for the choice of the wallpaper in our houses, the

behavior of animals, or the meteorological events – because the absence of meaning is disquieting.
- *the role of culture in the development of psychological functions*: psyche is not as universal as it seems. Psychic life and its ontogenetic development are situated in specific socio-historic and material contexts.
- *human agency, understood as both product and producer of culture*: human beings are not passive receivers of genetic or cultural heritage. People *participate* in cultures – that is, they act in the frame of already existing cultural practices (e.g., people do not merely feed, they eat dinner and breakfast), but they also constantly innovate those cultures through repeated everyday micro variations that can sometimes lead to major changes.
- *all systemic organism–environment relationships are units of analysis*: if human development is a dialogue of mutual adaptation and innovation between the person and the context, one cannot conceive an individual detached from the cultural context. However, because of the ubiquity of the cultural frame, we tend to "naturalize" and "neutralize" the role of environment that becomes transparent. Hence, the famous quote: "The fish will be the last to discover water" (Bruner, 1996, p. 45).
- *the genetic–historical and temporal dimension of psychological processes*: an axiom of cultural–historical approaches is that in order to understand a phenomenon we need to know about its genesis and development over time (see Chapter 2).

Giovan Battista Vico (1668–1744) was an Italian philosopher, rhetorician, historian, and jurist being the first expositor of the fundamentals of social science, philosophy of history, and semiotics.

Cultural psychology has a theoretical focus, and it criticizes the progressive detachment of psychology from human cultural phenomena, such as the complex intentional forms of feeling, thinking, and acting that characterize our everyday lives. "Scientific psychology" pursued the empirical accumulation of "hard" data by rewarding or punishing humans with tokens of food, money, etc. for taking part in laboratory experiments. Cultural psychology brings back the active persons in their real life settings who create, perform, and feel about food, theatre, poetry, and music, who read newspapers, get married, kill, care, etc. No human activity is explainable only by way of lower psychological functions, nor can be captured as simple variables or unpacked in simple behavioral, physiological, or cognitive dimensions. The study of complex psychological human phenomena requires adequate methodologies (Valsiner et al., 2016) (see Chapter 2).

Moritz Lazarus (1824–1903) was a German-Jewish philosopher and psychologist. He envisaged a *Völkerpsychologie* to study individual consciousness in the context of society as a whole. The psychologist must study the historical or comparative standpoint, analyzing the evolution of customs and conventions.

A BIT OF HISTORY

The Italian philosopher Giambattista Vico (Tateo, 2015) in the early 18th century was a pioneer in advocating the birth of a "new science", studying the relationship between mind and culture through the mediation of language, art, history, and religion. A century later, the systematic study of culture appears in the German philosophy of Wilhelm von Humboldt (1836), in the *Völkerpsychologie* of Moritz Lazarus in Bern (1859), and of Wilhelm Wundt in Leipzig (1879) later (Jahoda, 1993). The figure of Wundt dominated the historical narrative of psychology as a laboratory-experimental discipline that silenced the interest in cultural processes. Indeed, Wundt's biographies traditionally overlook the combination of both experimental and *Völkerpsychologie* traditions in his work. The general holistic, dynamic, and developmental emphasis was later developed by European traditions at the beginning of the 20th century: *Völkerpsychologie*; *Ganzheitspsychologie*; the introspection-based approach of the Würzburg School of Oswald Külpe; and the Austrian schools of Franz Brentano, and the Graz School of Alexius Meinong (see Chapter 5) (Diriwächter, 2004). In the second decade of the 20th century, Soviet cultural–historical psychology was initiated by Lev Vygotsky (see Chapter 1) and his circle, including scholars such as Lurja, Galperin, Leontev, Bernstein (Valsiner, 2012). The work of Vygotsky started to appear in the first, uncertain, English translations of his work in the 1960s. An ongoing critical rediscovery and the improvement of the translations (Van der Veer & Valsiner, 1991) turned the cultural–historical perspective into one of the most fruitful theoretical perspectives. The cultural–historical approach focuses on (see also Chapter 1 and 2 for the application of these principles):

- *the sociogenesis of the higher psychological functions*: all higher mental functions emerge as internalized social relationships.
- *the genetic epistemology*: psychological functions are historical.
- *the mediation of symbolic forms in all higher psychological functions*: the relationship between human mind and the world is mediated by signs and artifacts.
- *the whole of organism–environment relationship as unit of analysis in psychology*: psyche cannot be reduced to single components (memory, language, emotion, problem solving, etc.) of isolated individuals.
- *the notion of system of activity*: psychic life takes place in socio-cultural forms called contexts of activity. Activities preexist the individual life and are typical of each group (Brown, Heath & Pea, 1999).

Other contributions on the development of cultural psychology came from the so-called "culture and personality" tradition (Kluckhohn, Murray & Schneider, 1948) that established a dialogue between anthropology and psychology about the role of culture in shaping personality traits. The ideas of the Russian philosopher and literary critic Mikhail Bakhtin on psychology (see Chapter 2) led to the inclusion of the dialogical perspective (Clegg & Salgado, 2011) in cultural psychology. Jerome Bruner (1983; 1990) (see Chapter 1) stressed the centrality of meaning-making and cultural process in the psychological functioning and restored the dignity of the human mind as a relevant object of investigation.

Serge Moscovici (1925–2014) was a Romanian-born French social psychologist who developed the Theory of Social Representations and the Theory of Active Minorities. He was also one of the first psychologists actively involved in the ecological movement.

As Bruner (2012) pointed out:

I am deeply convinced that psychology cannot go it alone. The life of mind is not isolated from or independent of the life of the cultural community in which it develops and lives. Nor is it independent of the history that has shaped that cultural community. Our fate as human beings is shaped not only by our individual qualities but by the cultural circumstances in which we live our lives.

(2012, p. 12)

Human perception and cognition are embedded in culturally shared meanings (Bruner, 1990) and cannot be studied alone. The role of social interactions in cognitions is studied in the Theory of Social Representations by Serge Moscovici (Duveen, 1998; Sammut et al., 2015), focusing on common sense knowledge and the role of everyday communication in psychological functioning.

Due to its open, interdisciplinary, and critical nature, cultural psychology cannot be defined as a disciplinary or academic field. It is a particular way of looking at how human psyche develops in relation to value-laden, collectively coordinated, and symbolically mediated everyday activities. Cultural psychology is a special way of looking at human beings (Valsiner et al., 2016) in constant dialogue with other psychological perspectives such as socio-constructivism, phenomenology, and dynamic humanist psychology.

COLLECTIVE CULTURE AND PERSONAL CULTURE

Culture is not a container, culture has no agency, culture is not a box where one can place people. Nevertheless, everyone is intuitively aware that some people share a language, have similar tastes in food, believe in the same spiritual beings, have grown up together, etc. On the other hand, people feel a distance, a difference, from other groups of people. This feeling is so strong that one tends to believe that people can be categorized based on certain features and thus all people who share those features should be similar (culture as internally homogeneous). At a closer look, those things that people share, and which generally preexist the individual in the form of "contexts of activity", are not "injected" into people's minds but must go through several elaborations before becoming meaningful for the single person. The people who identify with the label of a common culture bear a "family resemblance" (Wittgenstein, 2001): although they seem connected by one essential common feature they may in fact be connected by a series of overlapping similarities, where no one feature is common to all of the persons. The "development of personal (subjective) and social (collective) domains of human experience" (Valsiner, 2014, 39) is coordinated but not isomorphic. Indeed, those domains are:

- *"CO-CONSTRUCTED": reconstructed in new forms between generations and cohorts of persons of the same age through a process of bi-directional communicative acts.*
- *"INTERNALIZED/EXTERNALIZED"* [see Chapter 1]: *persons actively decompose messages that are communicated to them by signs and recompose them into new intra-psychic patterns, and bring these patterns to the sphere of accessibility by others.*
- *"COORDINATED": different agents – persons, social institutions – regulate one another's experiencing of their life-worlds in ways that are directed but remain boundedly indeterminate.*

(Valsiner, 2014, 39)

Thus, culture is not a cake mold, shaped in the same way by people baking in the same kitchen. Neither is a stuffing injected into our mind through socialization. Culture is "in-between the person and the world" (Valsiner, 2014, p. 40). One can think of culture as a complex of meanings, artifacts, and practices that frame and guide the person's unique production and interpretation of meanings. The selective internalization of social messages – based on personal interests, expectations, imagination, fears, and desires – produces the unique dialogical and polyphonic (see Chapter 2) synthesis of a *personal culture* (Valsiner, 2014) that can bear family resemblances with other people.

WINDOW OF ACCEPTABLE POSSIBILITIES

The presence of collective culture is seldom felt as a coercive and violent pressure to act in a rigid and determined way. Apart from asylums and total institutions or for atrocious phenomena such as genocides, culture is present in the human environment in the form of signs codified according to a particular cultural context (Figure 3.5) that nudge toward (social suggestions) or inhibit (social constraints) certain types of potential conduct (Valsiner, 2014), sometimes with ambivalent messages (see Chapter 6).

Social suggestions are everywhere in the environment, constructing a complex network of signs that become *Gegenstanden* (see Chapter 1), and require the person to make sense of them. Social suggestions and social constraints set a frame of parameters, *a window of acceptable possibilities*, for what is preferable or not in a particular collective (Tateo, 2019a). Since early childhood, every person is required to selectively negotiate suggestions and constraints to find a personal developmental trajectory (Figure 3.6).

The window of acceptability operates according to cogenetic logic (see Chapter 1). Any social suggestion (e.g., "it is acceptable to do or to become X")

WHAT IS CULTURAL PSYCHOLOGY?

Figure 3.5 *A sign in a smoking room at Munich Airport (photo by Tateo, 2018)*

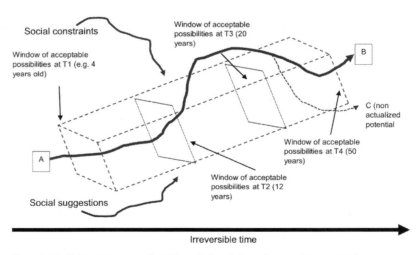

Figure 3.6 **Individual life course (A–B) through the window of acceptable possibilities**

immediately implies its negative impossibility (e.g., "is not acceptable to do or to become non-X"). Every culture can set different parameters during the life course and each person must negotiate her way through suggestions and constraints at some cost. The life course developmental milestones can vary but in general one can always identify cogenetic features, such as, for instance:

- learning goals at a given age + non-learning goals + the way to assess them: people are expected to learn things at a certain moment in life and they will be assessed somehow. Unacceptable learning goals in a certain culture can become acceptable within a sub-culture.
- appropriate behavior + non-appropriate behavior + the rules for observing it (when, how frequently, with whom, etc.): one of the most important things to learn is how to behave with other people. Nevertheless, it is also important to learn how far one can push the borders without becoming completely unacceptable (see Chapter 5).
- independence + non-independence + limits of the independence: this is one of the most important developmental aspects and it does not represent a liner trajectory. People can experience different degrees of interdependence in the life course. For instance, living in the parents' home as an adult is completely acceptable and encouraged in some cultures, while it is sign of failure in others.
- playtime + non-playtime + temporal border of playtime: one's control over life/work balance has become a central existential and psychological issue in the Global North. However, each culture has different parameters to define what is leisure and what is not, who is entitled to play, at what age, and when. Different cultures suggest the meaning of some activities and the acceptable age, whereas something that is considered as child participation to the family life can be considered as child labor from the point of view of another culture (Rogoff, 2003; Santana & Ristum, 2023).

Valsiner (2014) provides a good example of the dialogicality between personal culture and collective culture, speaking of fashion: "Fashion is a universal human cultural invention – it is functional as a cultural tool for creating our own personal cultures, as well as social distinctions" (Valsiner, 2014, p. 170). The outfit is a semiotic arena where a constant meaning negotiation takes place (Figure 3.7).

The person's outfit complies with the suggestions and constraints of culturally coded ways of dressing (suggested brands, combinations of clothing, body decorations, and accessories) with the goal of being unique. Fashion is about individuality in collectivity – the fashion market *consists of a serial production of differences.*

The outfit is part of both the person and the social environment. It is an interface (a semiotic mediator) that at the same time distances and connects the I–other relation (see Chapter 2). In a specific context of activity, the person engages in a dialogue involving one internal feed-forward loop that is coordinated with two social relations loops – ME < > ME and ME < > YOU (Figure 3.7) (Valsiner, 2014). On the one hand, the person engages in

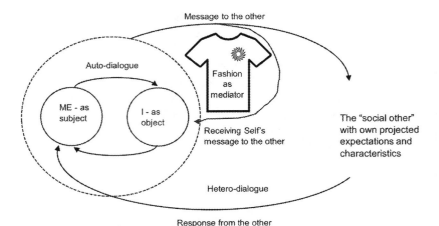

Figure 3.7 Semiotic mediation in the auto and heter-dialogue

a hetero-dialogue through sign mediation with the other, using the common code of fashion ("look at me, I am wearing X in my own personal way, so I am Y and you should respond Z"). On the other hand, the message to the other is also a message to the Self. It is an act of auto-regulation through sign mediation that says ("today I am wearing X and it makes me feel Y"). By wearing the clothes, the person is producing different layers of meaning and messages addressed *to the Self through the other* and *to the other through the Self*. In this example, the window of acceptable possibilities works by suggesting some parameters for what is acceptable or not as an outfit for a certain person. However, the fashion industry is nothing but a constant renegotiation and redefinition of the window of possibilities.

IN-BETWEEN CULTURES

Culture is neither a container the person belongs to, nor a content injected in the person's mind. Culture is a relationship of interdependency. It lives in the collective and coordinated process of relating with the environment and other human beings. The axiomatic indissolubility of the organism–environment whole as a dynamic totality (see Chapters 1 and 5) implies that a person does not just move from one cultural context to the other. As we discussed in the activity at the beginning of this chapter, the person is woven into a web of relationships between different, fuzzy bounded, and partially overlapping cultures and sub-cultures. What happens when the configuration of this network changes, for instance, following a migration?

A migration is an event that can take place at any moment in life, more or less planned, wanted, expected, or forced. It implies an encounter with different socio-cultural conditions, systems of value, ideas, semiotic codes, etc. (Gillespie, 2008). Most psychological theories understand the problem of transitioning from the native culture to the host culture as a matter of adaptation by acquiring a second culture that can potentially clash (marginalization), hybridize (acculturation), or replace (assimilation) the culture of origin (Gamsakhurdia, 2019a; 2019b). This perspective implies that there is not enough space in the mind for managing several cultures, which are static and cumbersome burdens the person is carrying. In cultural psychology, Gamsakhurdia (2019a; 2019b) developed an alternative perspective that described the elaboration of personal culture in relation to the experience of migration. Gamsakhurdia (2019a; 2019b) applied the principles of cultural psychology (see Chapter 1 and 2) to study the experience of migration as a process that unfolds in time, following a co-genetic logic, with a preparation phase, a transition, and a reconstruction of new meanings:

> Proculturation in emigration implies creative synthesis of unfamiliar signs in relation with familiar signs in the context of past and anticipated experiences and goals. Unlike acculturation, which implies development through orthogonal dimensions in direction or away from so-called heritage and foreign cultures, proculturation is a systemic process of the *self's curvilinear development and results in a construction of new fusions of meanings.*
>
> (Gamsakhurdia, 2019b, p. 168, emphasis in original)

A person is not a passive receiver of messages from old and new cultures. So, the process of transition cannot be reduced to a clash between conflicting social suggestions and constraints (see Figure 3.6). "Proculturative development is driven not only by the influence of foreign external stimuli, but also by striving for self-presentation into the environment" (Gamsakhurdia, 2019b, p. 169). The person is constructing their personal synthesis of the encounter with different cultural codes, values, practices, according to their goals and in relation to the window of acceptable possibilities. Not coincidentally, one of the most productive and visible forms of proculturation is food.

> However, it is not possible for humans to preserve elements of their lifestyle, values, or any other element of native cultural elements in the same/unaltered manner [. . .] due to the unavailability of particular conditions and due to the appearance of new circumstances. For example, Georgian emigrants cannot cook the Georgian dish Khachapuri in a traditional way anywhere outside Georgia, due to the unavailability of a specific Georgian cheese (Imeruli) [. . .]. So, they do not have any other choice but to use Western European sorts of cheese instead, which leads to the appearance of the new version of 'Europeanized' Khachapuri – the new form of this dish (which is essentially a new sign). So, this is another example when proculturation

leads to the creative mixture of elements representing home and host cultures.

(Gamsakhurdia, 2019b, p. 170)

The new sign of "Europeanized Khachapuri", which is not totally "Georgian" but neither totally "non-Georgian", becomes distinctive of a new personal identity of "Georgian outside Georgia" or "quasi-Georgian" (see Chapter 1), opening the way to the elaboration of a new field of meanings. Culture is no longer a static independent variable that affects the individual psyche but a repertoire of "symbolic resources" (Zittoun, 2006) that the person can use to create a personal synthesis. This makes impossible any type of direct cross-cultural comparison, as there is no such thing as a static, internally homogeneous, and measurable entity called "culture".

DECOLONIZING THE STUDY OF CULTURES

The term "cultural psychology" has often been used as a synonym for "cross-cultural psychology" (Heine, 2020; Heiphetz & Oishi, 2021), creating some confusion for students. The theories we discuss in this chapter are in dialectical opposition to the idea of universal psychological constructs, varying in magnitude, depending on the influence of culture understood as an independent variable (Anandalakshmi, 1974). If culture is not a variable, one cannot either create culture-free or context-independent methods and instruments to assess individual differences and aggregate them in abstract types (Cole, 2003). Cultural psychology rejects the universalistic perspective in psychology. On the contrary, psychological constructs are the product of "an indigenous psychology created out of a set of local cultural assumptions and values about the Western, individual self" (Bhatia, 2018, p. xxiii).

In this textbook, we introduce an ecological perspective that considers local reality as a complex ecosystem, whose unique relationships between the sub-parts cannot be replicated or exported. An understanding of the unique functioning of the local ecosystem can nevertheless produce generalizable knowledge about the process dynamics in ecological human systems that can become an interpretative tool for different local realities – a cultural ecosystem of different local experiences in neither a container nor an independent variable (Valsiner, 2014). Thus, there is no such a "thing" as an internally homogeneous American, Georgian, or Italian culture (generally overlapping with "national identity") that can cause effects on people's psyche or can be used to fully explain inter-group variability across people of the same age, gender, or status in two countries.

Culture is a frame, a configuration of relationships, and a process that human collectives develop to answer general existential questions (e.g., how we are born, reproduce, coordinate and manage conflicts, how we die, etc.). There can be as many answers as there are local ecosystems. Any

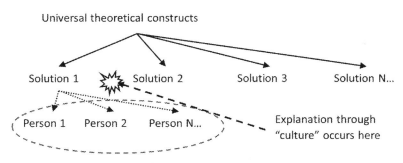

Figure 3.8 Current cross-cultural approach

cross-cultural comparison will probably just find some expected similarities and differences but no significant knowledge advancement (Figure 3.8).

The cross-cultural approach accumulates inductive evidence about personal variations of a cultural (national) pattern in relation to a hypothetical construct – as usually developed in a Western tradition – in two or more different local realities (Figure 3.8). Variability (or similarity) in a limited number of binary dimensions (e.g., dependence/independence/, collectivistic/individualistic, attachment styles, etc.) is explained by the person's belonging to the "culture". The generalization is not an outcome, but an assumption based on the universality of the construct itself. This is the target of decolonizing critique (Bhatia, 2018): constructs are not universal but they are the product of an indigenous, historically situated scientific tradition developed in the colonialist process.

AN ECOLOGICAL APPROACH TO MIND AND CULTURE

How can one construct general knowledge about the functioning of local cultural ecosystems? Starting from the theoretical (see Chapter 1) and methodological (see Chapter 2) principles of cultural psychology, one can generalize the process of finding answers to universal existential questions through personal and local syntheses (Figure 3.9).

The field of observation of cultural psychology is the whole (including every sub-part, both human and non-human elements) of the local reality, with a unique local configuration, the peculiar solution to existential problems that one can call "culture". People entertain with issues like "how to organize family relationships" or "how to differentiate myself from the other, but at the same time not to appear an alien". If one limits the comparison to two local solutions in different sites and times, one can just observe that people do a few things in a similar way and other things in a different way.

In an ecosystemic set of relationships, each person will instead construct her personal trajectory of existence, negotiating meanings, ambivalences

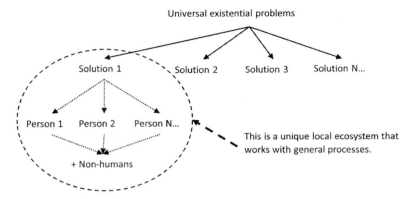

Figure 3.9 Ecosystemic approach to cultural differences

(see Chapter 6), and personal variations of values and conducts (Valsiner, 2014). This perspective has very important ethical implications. Voicing all the agents in the local ecosystem implies the commitment to "strong objectivity" (Harding, 2005). At the same time, the researcher entering in contact with the people in a research situation becomes part of the system.

THE ZONE OF POTENTIAL ESTRANGEMENT

The researcher is not a mere external and distant observer. If the local context is a set of mutual relationships between the sub-parts, then the act of researching establishes new relationships, creating a new sub-part (Tateo & Marsico, 2014). The illusion of "seeing without being seen" from an "objective" distance is a characteristic colonialist approach (Stewart, 2019). Doing research as capturing, explaining, selectively sampling, extracting is an act of silencing of the participants, especially those who are not in a position of power to produce an alternative discourse. Decolonizing and feminist perspectives have exposed and deconstructed the power relations in research activity that have silenced marginalized groups.

However, the researcher can sometimes fall into further different forms of asymmetric relationships:

a) the researcher can "speak on behalf of" the participant, when for instance she believes she is entitled to represent the instances of a marginalized group, while members of the group itself do not ask for someone to speak on their behalf, but require their own legitimate voice to be heard.
b) the researcher can "do the ventriloquist", attributing her personal, cultural, sometimes naïve, beliefs about the participants to the interpretation of their first person accounts.

Voicing the participants is not a straightforward or neutral action. The first-person perspective, which is crucial in critical and decolonizing epistemologies, can be a delusion as much as pure objectivity. Any attempt to provide an interpretation of reality without including the researcher as part of the ecosystem will fail. The act of research leaves an ecological footprint in the system, creating tension, resistance, and a need for negotiation.

The researcher in cultural psychology works in the zone of potential estrangement (ZPE): "the dialogical gaining of mutual awareness between the actors involved in the research interaction that knowledge is not representation rather interpretation" (Tateo, 2019b, p. 150). The act of researching is part of a process that goes from the selection of the phenomenon to understanding the basis of the researcher's educated insight (see Chapter 2) and continues until the act of narrating that experience. During the process, the researcher has the power of silencing, ventriloquing, or speaking on behalf of the other. The act of reporting the research outcomes is not a neutral representation of a "real" situation. It consists of naturalizing the position of observer through some pre-existing conceptual tools. The ecological epistemology of cultural psychology is respectful of the local ecosystem but derives a universal specimen of a form of life (Figure 3.14). This is different from sampling a general class of phenomena:

> It is experiencing a unique moment: a single case in everyday experience. On the other hand, any capturing is a form of violence, and it is transformational. In the pure inductive mode of thought, one can believe that it is just a matter of precision: the more my picture-measuring is accurate, the more my understanding.
>
> (Tateo, 2019b, p. 151)

The researcher is a person with an educated, selective, perspective yet privileged position, theoretical understanding, and specific observation skills. However, the researcher also has a personal identity project. Starting from this position, the researcher establishes a new relationship with the local ecosystem that results in the understanding (or misunderstanding) of that specific and unique situation.

An observation is not a re-presentation. It is rather a creative production of a specimen that helps the researcher to gain abductive understanding of the phenomenon (Figure 3.10). In a portrait, the artist does not re-present the "reality" of a person as in a "mirror" (Bhatia, 2018). The painter rather takes a life experience, manipulates it through artistic method, and gives back a new experience for the public. In the uncanny space between the original subject of the work and the experience of the spectators lies a zone of estrangement. It is the power of the work of art to open new spaces of understanding. In this process, the artist conveys her own point of view as well as that of the historical moment in which the work is created. There is no binary

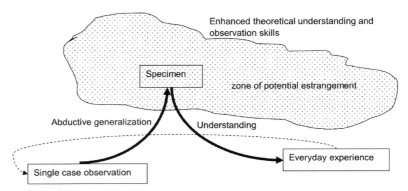

Figure 3.10 Abductive generalization, understanding, and zone of potential estrangement

opposition between the voice of the represented person and the voice of the artist: the result is a dialogue between the two.

In cultural psychology, the starting point is not the inductive accumulation of empirical instances, rather the abductive process of grasping the complexities of human psychic experience. The researcher's participation in the local ecosystem implies a continuous movement of approaching and distancing. Every act of approaching and distancing implies a different understanding of the phenomenon. It is neither assessing based on an external standard nor naively mirroring the phenomenon (Bhatia, 2018). The researcher "abducts" the phenomenon, brings it into their personal perspective, and gives it back as new forms of understanding (Figure 3.10). The movement of approaching and distancing allows the emergence of a *space of estrangement*. The ZPE is "a field of open meanings that emerges in between the act of exploring everyday experience and the act of telling everyday experience" (Tateo, 2019b, 151).

SUMMARY OF CHAPTER 3

In Chapter 3, we have discussed the concept of culture in relation to the human psyche. We have defined cultural psychology as the study of third-level psychological processes. We have defined culture as a process and configuration of relationships. The permanence and cultivation of those relationships constitutes the "cultural" in cultural psychology. Then, we identified the basic focus of cultural psychology:

- the centrality of the meaning-making processes
- the role of culture in the development of psychological functions
- human agency, understood as both product and producer of culture

- all systemic organism–environment relationships as a unit of analysis
- the genetic–historical and temporal dimensions of psychological processes.

We then presented the relationship between collective culture and personal culture, and described what happens in a person's transition between cultures, using the concept of *proculturation*.

We have discussed the differences in the cross-cultural approach and claimed that culture is not an independent variable. Finally, we presented the critiques to the psychological study of culture within the decolonizing perspective and the ethical implications, presenting the concept of the zone of potential estrangement.

Check your knowledge and reflect

Task: After reading this chapter, choose a phenomenon of your interest in everyday life (e.g., young people's romantic relationships; family rituals at the dinner table; your favorite type of music; racial discrimination in your society; etc.) and try to reflect on what you have learned by writing a short essay (maximum two pages) elaborating your personal view and using the concepts presented so far. Then, share your essay with two colleagues and ask for their feedback.

REFERENCES

Aass Solbakken, B., Wikborg Wiese, K., Hove Solberg, I. & Husby, T. (Eds.) (2024). *Dragons and logs*. Oslo: Nasjonalmuseet.

Anandalakshmi, S. (1974). How independent is the independent variable? Problems and perspectives from New Delhi. In J. L. M. Dawson & W. J. Lonner (Eds.), Readings in cross-cultural psychology (pp. 79–89). Hong Kong: Hong Kong University Press.

Anderson, B. (1991) *Imagined communities: Reflections on the origin and spread of Nationalism*, 2nd edition. New York: Verso.

Bhatia, S. (2018). *Decolonizing psychology*. New York: Oxford University Press.

Boas, F. (1904). The history of anthropology. *Science*, *20*(512), 513–524.

Boesch, E. E. (1991). *Symbolic action theory and cultural psychology*. Berlin: Springer-Verlag. https://doi.org/10.1007/978-3-642-84497-3

Brown, J. S., Heath, C., & Pea, R. (1999). *Perspectives on activity theory*. New York: Cambridge University Press.

Bruner, J. S. (1983). *In search of mind: Essays in autobiography*. New York: Harper & Row.

Bruner, J. (1990). *Acts of meaning*. Cambridge, MA: Harvard University Press.

Bruner, J. S. (1996). The Culture of Education. Cambridge, MA: Harvard University Press.

Bruner, J. (2012). What psychology should study. *International Journal of Educational Psychology*, *1*(1), 5–13.

Ciofalo, N. (Ed.). (2019). *Indigenous psychologies in an era of decolonization*. New York: Springer International Publishing.

Clegg, J. W., & Salgado, J. (2011). From Bakhtinian theory to a dialogical psychology. *Culture & Psychology*, *17*(4), 520–533.

Cole, M. (2003). *Cultural psychology: A once and future discipline*, 6th edition. Cambridge, MA: Harvard University Press.

Cole, M., & Packer, M. (2016). A bio-cultural-historical approach to the study of development. *Handbook of Advances in Culture and Psychology*, 6, 1–75.

Cornejo, C., Marsico, G., & Valsiner, J. (Eds.). (2018). *I activate you to affect me*. Charlotte, NC: Information Age Publishers.

Descola, P. (2013). *Beyond nature and culture*. Chicago, IL: Chicago University Press.

Diriwächter, R. (2004). Völkerpsychologie: The synthesis that never was. *Culture & Psychology*, 10(1), 85–109. https://doi.org/10.1177/1354067X04040930

Duveen, G. (1998). The psychosocial production of ideas: Social representations and psychologic. *Culture & Psychology*, 4(4), 455–472.

Gamsakhurdia, V. L. (2019a). Making identity, proculturation in-between Georgianness and Westernness. *Human Arenas*, 2(3), 356–377. https://doi.org/10.1007/s42087-019-00062-0

Gamsakhurdia, V. L. (2019b). Proculturation: Self-reconstruction by making "fusion cocktails" of alien and familiar meanings. *Culture & Psychology*, 25(2), 161–177.

Gillespie, A. (2008). Social representations, alternative representations and semantic barriers. *Journal for the Theory of Social Behaviour*, 38(4), 375–391. https://doi.org/10.1111/j.1468-5914.2008.00376.x.

Harding, S. (2005). Rethinking standpoint epistemology: What is "strong objectivity?" In A. E. Cudd & R. O. Andreasen (Eds.), Feminist theory: A philosophical anthology (pp. 49–73). Oxford: Blackwell Publishing.

Heine, S. J. (2020). *Cultural psychology*, 4th International Student Edition. New York: WW Norton & Company.

Heiphetz, L., & Oishi, S. (2021). Viewing development through the lens of culture: Integrating developmental and cultural psychology to better understand cognition and behavior. *Perspectives on Psychological Science*. Online first, July 2021, https://doi.org/10.1177/1745691620980725

Humboldt, W. von. (1988 [1836]). *Über die Verschiedenheit des menschlichen Sprachbaues und ihren Einfluss auf die geistige Entwickelung des Menschengeschlechts. – Wilhelm von Humboldt's gesammelte Werke. Kuudes nide*. Berlin: Walter de Gruyter.

Klempe, S. H. (2021). *Sound and reason*. New York: Palgrave.

Kluckhohn, C., Murray, H. A., & Schneider, D. M. (Eds.). (1948). *Personality in nature, society, and culture*, 2nd review edition. New York: Knopf.

Kroeber, A. L., & Kluckhohn, C. (1952). Culture: A critical review of concepts and definitions. Papers. *Peabody Museum of Archaeology & Ethnology, Harvard University*, 47(1), viii, 223.

Kull, K. (1998). Semiotic ecology: Different natures in the semiosphere. *Σημειωτκή-Sign Systems Studies*, 26(1), 344–371.

Jahoda, G. (1993). *Crossroads between culture and mind: Continuities and change in theories of human nature*. Cambridge MA: Harvard University Press.

Lewontin, R. C. (2000). *The triple helix: Gene, organism, and environment*. Cambridge, MA: Harvard University Press.

Rogoff, B. (2003). *The cultural nature of human development*. New York: Oxford University Press.

Sammut, G. E., Andreouli, E. E., Gaskell, G. E., & Valsiner, J. E. (2015). *The Cambridge handbook of social representations*. Cambridge, MA: Cambridge University Press.

Santana, R. R. C., & Ristum, M. (2023). Among risks, protection, and lessons learned: Perspectives of Brazilian rural families about work in adolescence. *Journal of Research on Adolescence*, 00, 1–14. https://doi.org/10.1111/jora.12903

Shweder, R. A. (1991). *Thinking through cultures: Expeditions in cultural psychology*. Cambridge MA: Harvard University Press.

Stewart, S. (ed.) (2019). *Decolonizing qualitative approaches for and by the Caribbean*. Charlotte, NC: Information Age Publishing.

Tateo, L. (2015). Giambattista Vico and the principles of cultural psychology: A programmatic retrospective. *History of the Human Sciences, 28*(1), 44–65.

Tateo, L. (2018). Nature unveiling herself before science. In G. Jovanović, L. Allolio-Näcke, & C. Ratner (Eds.). The challenges of cultural psychology: Historical legacies and future responsibilities (pp. 59–74). London: Routledge.

Tateo, L. (2019a). The inherent ambivalence of educational trajectories and the zone of proximal development with reduced potential. In L. Tateo (Ed.), *Educational dilemmas* (pp. 1–21). London: Routledge.

Tateo, L. (2019b). Caravaggio's *The Seven Works of Mercy* and the art of generalization. In C. Højholt & E. Schraube (Eds.), *Subjectivity and knowledge* (pp. 141–156). Cham, Switzerland: Springer.

Tateo, L., & Marsico, G. (2014). Open complementarity in cultural psychology. In B. Wagoner, N. Chaudhary, & P. Hviid (Eds.), *Culture psychology and its future: Complementarity in a new key* (pp. 77–91). Charlotte, NC: Information Age Publications.

Tateo, L., & Marsico, G. (2023). Sensing the city: Affective semiosis and urban border-zones. In S. Petrilli and C. Ji (Eds.), *Intersemiotic perspectives on emotions. Translating across signs, bodies and values* (pp. 196–209). London: Routledge.

Valsiner, J. (2014). *An invitation to cultural psychology.* London: Sage.

Valsiner, J. (2019). *Culture & Psychology*: 25 constructive years. *Culture and Psychology, 25*(4), 429–469.

Valsiner, J. E. (Ed.) (2012). *The Oxford handbook of culture and psychology.* New York: Oxford University Press.

Valsiner, J., Marsico, G., Chaudhary, N., Sato, T., & Dazzani, V. (2016). *Psychology as the science of human being.* The Yokohama Manifesto. New York: Springer

Van der Veer, R., & Valsiner, J. (1991). *Understanding Vygotsky: A quest for synthesis.* Oxford: Blackwell Publishing.

Vermeersch, E. (1978). An analysis of the concept of culture. In B. Bernardi (Ed.), *The concept and dynamics of culture* (pp. 9–74). The Hague: De Gruyter. https://doi.org/10.1515/9783110807745.9

Wagoner, B., Brescó, I., & Awad, S. H. (2019). *Remembering as a cultural process.* Cham, Switzerland: Springer.

Wertsch, J. V., del Rio, P., & Alvarez, A. (Eds.). (1995). *Sociocultural studies of mind.* Cambridge: Cambridge University Press. https://doi.org/10.1017/CBO9781139174299

Williams, G. (2023). Far more happier than we Europeans: Reactions to the Australian Aborigines on Cook's voyage. In *Buccaneers, explorers and settlers* (pp. 499–512). London: Routledge.

Wittgenstein, L. (2001). *Philosophical investigations.* London: Blackwell Publishing.

Zittoun, T. (2006). *Transitions: Development through symbolic resources.* Greenwich (CT): InfoAge.

CHAPTER 4 # Imagination

Scan the QR-code to access additional materials and watch outstanding international scholars discussing key concepts.

> **LEARNING GOALS**
>
> 1. To acquire the concept of imaginative process as higher mental function
> 2. To understand the way cultural psychology conceptualizes human imagination
> 3. To understand how imagination works in future-oriented meaning-making

CHAPTER OVERVIEW

In this chapter, we discuss the role of imagination among psychological functions. Then, we present two main theories of imagination in cultural psychology and how imagination works in everyday life.

GROUP ACTIVITIES FOR INSTRUCTOR

Activity 1: Do you know your body?

The instructor asks the students to measure their own internal organs (heart, liver, kidney, etc.). How big are they? Where are they located exactly? They can touch themselves and try to identify the organs, their position, borders, shape, etc. Do they work properly? Then, the instructor asks the students to focus on the exact position of their body, to figure out the position of your limbs, how weight and force are distributed. They try to visualize the exact position of their bones, to catch the feeling of tension and relaxation. They try to become aware of the energy required in the event of changing position. Students can close their eyes for a while if needed. Then, they take some time to reflect upon the thoughts, images and feelings aroused. For instance, the instructor can ask: How do you represent your body? How do you feel or visualize your limbs, the inner parts? How do you know what is your exact position while sitting?

Activity 2: Taking pictures

The students can work individually or in small groups. They go around the campus and take a picture of one or more of the following things: culture, love, god, intelligence, atmosphere, justice, taste, time, happiness, health, youth, freedom. The instructor can of course change the list or add any concept to adapt to the local context. After a few minutes (at least 15–20 minutes) the students come back to the classroom and share their images. They take turns to show their pictures and explain why they choose to capture each of them (e.g., "What pictures did you take? Why?"). After a first round of presentations, the instructor asks to the students to point to where in the image one can see the thing (e.g., "In that picture, can you point exactly where is god, or love, etc.?"). The instructor will stimulate students to reflect on the fact that some ideas we use in everyday life do not have an ontological correspondence and can be visualized symbolically or consensually attributed to objects that represent them. Nevertheless, those "non-existing objects" play a very important role in individual and collective life, such as the concept of freedom or love.

Reflection questions

The activity is aimed at experiencing the relationship between imagining and knowing, and how we use both imaginative and non-imaginative modalities to make sense of ourselves and the world around us. Some trigger questions for reflecting are:

- How do you know the inside of your body? Where does that knowledge come from?
- How do you know if something is a product of your imagination or a product of your epistemic activity?
- When do you use imagination in everyday life – can you provide all the examples that come to mind?

DO WE KNOW OR DO WE IMAGINE?

In 1969, the Evangelic priest and amateur gastronomist Robert Farrar Capon published an interesting book titled *The Supper of the Lamb* (Capon, 2002) mixing philosophy, gastronomy, and religion. The author reported an interesting humoristic parable that is worth citing extensively:

> Satan was upset and convened the council of Hell. 'What are we doing to speed up dehumanization of mankind?'. All the heads of Departments, Luxury, War, Avarice, Envy, Pride made excellent and prolix states of advancement. But Satan got bored and thumping the table shouted: 'The same stupid chatting! Nobody has new ideas?'. The youngest devil raised the hand and said: 'We should create the Department of Desubstantiation. We failed because we didn't address the essence of humanity, that is the relationship with concrete objects that give pleasure and surprise, providing energy to mankind. We should replace concrete things and beings with their abstractions, schemes, spiritualizations. Things will no longer be an end in themselves but shall have a symbolic value, they shall serve to something else'. 'Excellent!' said Satan, 'let's go ahead!'
>
> (Capon, 2022, pp. 106–107)

The short story raises an interesting question: what is the nature of the human relationship with the world? As we know from Chapters 1 and 2, this relationship is mediated by signs and artifacts. Yet, human beings are also able to relate to abstractions affectively. In our everyday experience, we deal with things that can be touched, smelled, heard, seen in first person. We also do things for love, honor, pride, duty, religious beliefs, that cannot be experienced through senses because they are abstractions, but for us they are as real as a piece of bread (Tateo, 2020). We know something about the things we experience directly, in a proximal way, but also about the things of which we have no direct experience, such as a distant country, something in the past before we were born, or in the future, that is we have *distal* experiences (Zittoun & Gillespie, 2015).

As we saw in the first activity, it is not possible to directly access all the parts that our bodies – the organs, bones, muscles etc. – are made up of. In a certain sense, the only way to achieve such knowledge is by mediation. What does this mediation consist of? We can use previous knowledge acquired through education and media, using the images and anatomical representations of the body we have learned. We can use the knowledge of other people, who have told us how the body is constructed, assuming all human bodies are similar. Those are all symbolic resources (Zittoun & Gillespie, 2015) available to a given community, such as stories or paintings (Figure 4.1). At the same time, we must use some form of imaginative work when it comes to accessing our own body here and now. "Without imagination, nothing in the world could be meaningful. Without imagination, we could never make sense of our experience. Without imagination, we could never reason toward knowledge of reality" (Johnson, 2013, p. ix). In sum, it seems that our experience of the world and of ourselves is a combination of imaginative and non-imaginative parts. Moreover, the axiomatic assumptions of cultural psychology are that (a) we experience through purposefully establishing affective relationships with the world, and (b) meaning-making emerges from the need to proactively adapt to future environmental conditions in relation to our purposes. Human psychological life is oriented toward what is currently not yet known, asking "what's next"?

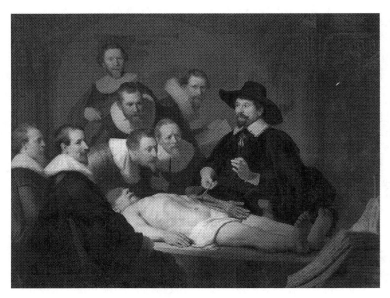

Figure 4.1 Rembrandt van Rijn, *The Anatomy Lesson of Dr. Nicolaes Tulp* (*ca.*1632) (https://commons.wikimedia.org/wiki/File:Rembrandt_-_The_Anatomy_Lesson_of_Dr_Nicolaes_Tulp.jpg)

KNOWING BY IMAGINING

Everyone can observe that, as a matter of general opinion, there are some things one can be more certain about whilst others are less certain. One can represent this phenomenological field as a round bubble with the person at its center. Such a perceptive/effective bubble constitutes the *Umwelt* of any living system (von Uexküll, 2013). If one could have the same degree of certainty about all the events in the surrounding world, the bubble would have a perfectly spherical shape. In any direction one looks, one could have the same degree of certainty about the truth of one's beliefs and expectations.

However, in real life one never has the same knowledge or magnitude of certainty about everything. Indeed, there are some things one can be sure about only to a certain extent, some things about which one can be 99% sure, whilst others are less sure or not sure at all. For instance, one can be sure about my telling the truth – or not – about something, to a certain degree. But one can have a different degree of confidence in my partner (or a politician!) telling the truth.

The bubble of life world extends in every direction. So, the degree of certainty is also inscribed in irreversible time (see Chapter 1). One can probably be more confident about things in the past and less sure about what is going to happen in the future. This is independent of the means we use to produce any inference about the life world. Simply, there are things in one's life world about which statements with a different degree of confidence can be made (Tateo, 2015). It doesn't matter if knowledge is based on experience, habit, guess, or induction, etc. The world one experiences has regions with different degrees of certainty. Thus, it cannot be represented as a perfect spherical bubble. It has a rather irregular shape, in which "me" as a knower occupies a decentered position (Figure 4.2).

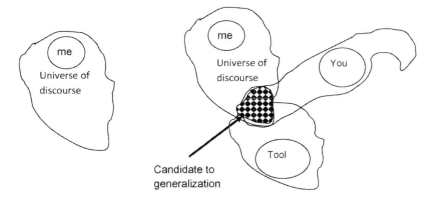

Figure 4.2 Portions of universe and potential generalization

Every time one encounters a new phenomenon in life, the shape of the life world is subject to change.

The problem that a positive or negative encounter with an unfamiliar object poses for an individual is just the problem of inferring the consequential region to which that object belongs.
(Shepard, 1987, p. 1319)

Figure 4.2 is bi-dimensional. Nevertheless, we have to figure it as a tridimensional space, extending in all directions and including the orthogonal relation between past and future and abstract and concrete. For instance, one can be more sure about the concrete feelings of pain/pleasure, and less sure about the abstract concepts of pain/pleasure. This is why people often use concrete images to "give a body", a metaphorical presence, to the abstract concepts (see activity 2 above). One can be more sure about events happening in a certain temporal flow ("the sun will rise again tomorrow"), and less sure about things in the future ("I will win the lottery").

How do people improve their degree of knowledge and confidence about the world? How do we fill the gaps in our experience of the world? To overcome the limitations of our own beliefs, we do a very simple thing: we turn to others or to some instruments that can provide more knowledge. This is true in everyday life as well as in scientific practice.

We then turn to others in order to strengthen our knowledge about the different parts of the portion of discourse universe, involving the socially organized forms of intersubjectivity and interobjectivity we use to call scientific inquiry.
(Tateo, 2015, p. 58)

The squared area in Figure 4.2 represents the portion of the life world in which the first-person experience, others' knowledge, and cultural tools are combined to create a potential zone of reliable knowledge. For instance, one can find one's way around a city center by relying on a combination of one's own sense of orientation, asking other people for directions, and using a map to be sure of following the right path. All three modalities will converge to provide some more or less solid belief in being able to not get lost. Even within the region of the life world which is closer to that "me" as knower, more familiar, one realizes that any form of new knowledge is attained with the mediation of the others or of tools: experience is always socially and culturally mediated. Social interaction and cultural resources are forms of vicarious experience already described by Vygotsky (2004). Also when vicarious experience contributes to the expansion of our field of knowledge, the degree of confidence is different and largely determined by social factors, such as trust: I can believe more or less in the narrative of another person depending on how much I trust them.

Once the new portion of the life world is rendered denser by social and cultural mediation (Figure 4.2), it becomes a potential candidate for generalization (Tateo, 2015).

> We generalize from one situation to another not because we cannot tell the difference between the two situations but because we judge that they are likely to belong to a set of situations having the same consequence.
> (Shepard, 1987, p. 1322)

This is the mechanism of peer-reviewing in science. To improve the degree of certainty about a new portion of scientific discourse (e.g., a manuscript or a study), an intersubjective process is used to validate the portion of life world as a candidate for a potential new scientific generalization of the knowledge produced. Sciences have of course formalized, explicit, and replicable procedures through which the different subjects can share knowledge about specific portions of the life world.

However, there are limits to the experience based on socio-cultural mediation. What happens when one must look ahead, make plans, foresee alternative futures, make hypotheses? In other words, how can one fill the gaps otherwise? Two theories of imagination have recently been developed in the framework of cultural psychology: the theory of uncoupling (Zittoun & Gillespie, 2015), and the theory of imaginative process as higher mental function (Tateo, 2020).

IMAGINATION AS UNCOUPLING

Zittoun and Gillespie (2015) used the metaphor of "uncoupling" to describe imagination as a socio-cultural phenomenon. According to them, human experience unfolds on a stream of experience guided by the immediate social and material world and a stream of imagination. Imagination is a way of temporarily distancing the person from the immediate here-and-now and engaging with alternative, distal experiences, which are not subject to linear or causal temporality (Zittoun & Gillespie, 2015). During the decoupling experience, the person has sufficient space to explore, simulate, experiment with, create, etc. (Figure 4.3).

> An imagination event thus begins with a decoupling of experience and usually concludes with a re-coupling. Thus, imagination is a loop. Imagination as a looping experience, as a temporary disengagement from current experience, can account for phenomena such as daydreaming, creating, deciding, remembering, having a cultural experience, and so on. These are all experiences which can be emotionally intense, intellectually challenging, and which can change us, without necessarily affecting other people or our environment.
> (Zittoun & Gillespie, 2015, p. 40)

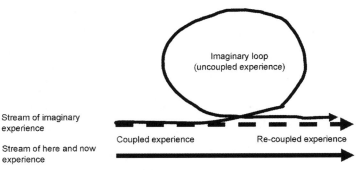

Figure 4.3 Imagination as a loop (Zittoun & Gillespie, 2015)

The imaginary loop can be triggered by different conditions. According to Zittoun and Gillespie (2015), people can disengage from reality when the established meaning in everyday life is questioned or disrupted. When people experience ruptures (Zittoun, 2006) – that is more or less serious breakdown of taken for granted knowledge that needs to be made sense of – they use imagination to produce new tools, images, or representations to adjust to the change. Also, *boredom* or *overstimulation* may trigger a detachment from the here and now, as for instance in the case of *mind-wandering* (Dario & Tateo, 2022). If people needed to solve a task or a find a solution, they can voluntarily loop in and out of the here and now situation, as for instance during creative work, writing, inventing, or brainstorming (Vygotsky, 2004).

Finally, people can purposefully strive for activities in which voluntary uncoupling is culturally organized, like in the case of collective rituals, use of psychotropic substances, theater, and cinema. Of course, the triggers can be combined in different ways (e.g., boredom can lead to substances use, or ruptures can lead to searching for meaning in artistic productions, etc.). Anyway, imagination is culturally guided through the practices and shared symbolic resources available in a particular context.

IMAGINING FUTURE WORLDS: MENTAL EXPERIMENTS AND UTOPIAS

The commonsense idea about imagination is that it corresponds to an alternative to reality, an escape, a fairy world, a fantasy. We have instead presented examples of how imagination is related to knowing. Many scientific theories started with mental experiments based on human imaginative activity (McAllister, 2012). The different forms of complementarity between imaginative and non-imaginative modes of thought are crucial to scientific work. According to Mc Allister:

> Scientists use imagination in this sense when they conceive possible features of the world that they have not previously encountered empirically.

Imagination is involved whenever scientists posit unobserved, unobservable, or nonactual states of affairs, such as in conjectures, counterfactual reasoning, predictions, models, and idealizations, as well as in thought experiments.

(McAllister, 2012, p. 11)

Mental experiments imply the complementarity between what one already knows – because one has inductively or deductively produced some knowledge – and what one doesn't yet know – because it has not yet been encountered empirically. A mental experiment produces an abductive inference[1] based on the production of a completely new element, an overcoming of the current situation, not just a recombination of existing elements in a creative way. According to Lapoujade (1988), it is precisely the work of imagination that sets the limits of knowledge whilst at the same time denying those limits by offering a glimpse of their overcoming.

Let's take for instance Einstein's famous "elevator on a rope" mental experiment (Cropper, 2001; Norton, 2012). This was one of the most important mental experiments that paved the way for modern physics. In its visionary complexity, it cannot be reduced to the manipulation of mental images or the recombination of previous experiences. Indeed, the initial almost "ordinary" condition – a man in a falling elevator – became more and more "visionary" as the different possible conditions – not empirically observable – were explored. Einstein's second step was to imagine the elevator upward in constant acceleration along an infinite rope rising in the sky. Then he introduced an even more visionary element:

Picture the elevator on a rope with a light ray traveling across the elevator from left to right [. . .] Because the light ray takes a finite time to travel from wall to wall, and the elevator is accelerated upward during that time, the outside observer sees the light ray traveling the slightly curved path shown.

(Cropper, 2001, p. 221)

Another example is found in the biography of Stephen Hawking (White & Gribbin, 2002). During his doctorate at Cambridge, Hawking, his supervisor, and some colleagues went to King's College in London to attend a lecture on the mathematician Roger Penrose. This is how White and Gribbin (2002) reported the episode:

One night, on the way back to Cambridge, they were all seated together in a second-class compartment and had begun to discuss what had been said at the meeting that evening. Feeling disinclined to talk for a moment, Hawking peered through the window, watching the darkened fields stream past and the juxtaposition of his friends reflected in the glass. His colleagues were arguing over one of the finer mathematical points in Penrose's discussion. Suddenly, an idea struck him, and he looked away from the window. Turning to Sciama sitting across from him, he said, 'I wonder what would happen if you applied Roger's singularity theory to the entire Universe.' In the event it was that single idea that saved Hawking's Ph.D. and set him on the road to science superstardom.

(White & Gribbin, 2002, pp. 71–72)

From Hawking's imaginative exercise, one can see how the mental experiment is "*a complementary work of imaginative and non-imaginative activity focusing on a specific problem that goes beyond the current limits of the universe of discourse*" (Tateo, 2020, p. 41, emphasis in original) (Figure 4.4).

If a mental experiment is not focusing on a specific problem but on a whole universe of discourse, it can be considered a *utopia* (Miščević, 2012). In the case of the utopia, the complementarity between imaginative and non-imaginative work is extended to cover a whole system in its political, social, ethical, and affective dimensions. Mental experiments and utopias show how imaginative work is not an incidental element that sometimes comes to interfere with or enrich a work of rationality. Imagining is a necessary, though not sufficient, condition for any new understanding (Figure 4.4). Imaginative and non-imaginative work constantly feed into each other.

Following Vygotsky's theory (2004), the imaginative mode of thinking is involved in scientific work because it has the same origin, the internalized social interactions, of the non-imaginative one.

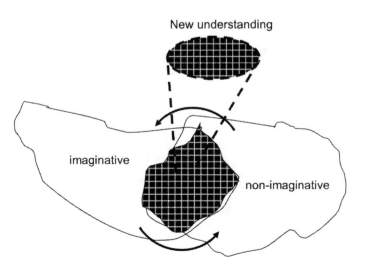

Figure 4.4 Imaginative and non-imaginative activity

EXPANSIVE AND REDUCTIVE IMAGINATION

The word imagination derives from the Latin word *imago*, which has several meanings: image, imitation, likeness, statue, representation, ancestral image, ghost, apparition, semblance, appearance, shadow, echo, conception, thought, reminder, depiction. All those meanings still feed into the current definitions of imagination. Carl Gustav Jung (1959) directly used the original Latin term *imago*: "to qualify a fact of experience as psychic and to suspend judgment with regard to its possible reference to any state of affairs in the so-called objective world, physical or metaphysical" (Heisig, 1976, p. 91).

According to Jung (1959), the plan of imagination is a psychological truth somehow superimposed on reality, with the production of a phantasmatic scheme that becomes a guiding pattern in our interpretation of the Other. One usually considers imagination as something that *expands* reality and its possibilities. But imagination can also have an inhibitory and reductive function (Tateo, 2017; 2023) of personal and social control (Figure 4.5).

Karl Gustav Jung (1875–1961) was a Swiss psychiatrist and psychoanalyst who founded analytical psychology. He was a prolific author, illustrator, and correspondent.

Figure 4.5 Wall painting from the South Germany school, author unknown, 18th century (https://commons.wikimedia.org/wiki/File:Tot_und_lebendig.jpg)

The inhibitory function of imaginative activity is well known by every organized religion. Figure 4.5 is an example of a common religious genre in Christianity: the *memento mori* (Latin for "remember you are going to die"). The painting represents the classical theme of death and the maiden. The young pretty and happy girl on the left side is holding a flower, symbol of beauty and life but also of its caducity. The dead half on the right is holding an arrow, symbol of the inevitability and sudden way in which death can strike amid the flourishing of life. The cartouche at the top of the figure reads: *"Remember, O Man, Look who you are/How unequal Dead and Alive are"*. Since the Middle Ages, the *memento mori* was ubiquitous in churches, private and public places of gathering, cemeteries, etc. Its function was to constantly remind people of the fugacity of life and the necessity of living in preparation for God's judgment. Nowadays, one can hardly imagine how a person surrounded by those images of death could live. Contemporary Western societies are indeed exorcising the idea of one's own death while producing images of war and catastrophes happening to *Others* (Tateo, 2019). The internalization of proliferating *memento mori* could produce two opposite but complementary responses – either a powerful inhibitory mechanism of "sinful" conduct or a strong encouragement to enjoy life exactly because of its ephemeral nature. Thus, the cultural artifact worked as a mediational tool in imaginative work to regulate real life conduct. In other words, reality must also be assessed *against* imagination, both in its reductive and expansive functions.

THE THEORY OF IMAGINATIVE PROCESS AS A HIGHER MENTAL FUNCTION

Most theories of imagination have captured different aspects of this polymorphic and complex feature of the human psyche but fell short when locating imaginative activity in relation to other higher mental functions. Without imaginative activity, our world would be flattened here and now (Zittoun & Gillespie, 2015) like that of a fly (von Uexküll, 2013). Every individual weaves a web of relations with the properties of surrounding things, which constitutes their world (*Umwelt*). This is the space of selected and secure perceived features in which the individual can manage to build effective responses. It is the realm of known paths of experiencing and actions produced by personal elaborations.

The limits of this web of relations is the border between what von Uexküll (2013) called the *Umwelt* and the environment (*Umgebung*[2]). The ordering power of the individual is exerted on a selected part of the life world. What is outside the perception/action field constitutes a realm of uncertainty and danger, though still part of the environment. Human beings constantly strive to explore the *Umgebung*, and incorporate it into the *Umwelt* through transformative (and sometimes destructive) meaningful conducts.

Jakob Johann Freiherr von Uexküll (1864–1944) was a German-Estonian biologist, influential on the cybernetics of life. His most notable contribution is the notion of *Umwelt*. His works established the field of biosemiotics.

Human beings experience and know their world through culturally mediated complementarity between imaginative and non-imaginative activity. The *Umwelt* is constructed from the subjective perspective of the individual, rich in both imaginative and non-imaginative overlapping features: in this sense, every personal world is partly "magic" (von Uexküll, 2013).

Many people have probably experienced being home alone and suddenly feeling a shadow, or a sound in the peripherical perceptual field. One feels the "presence" of some "being", something just ran to hide behind a corner, although there is no visible trace. This is indeed a "trick" of perception, but one keeps a sense of unease and alert when entering the room again. Von Uexküll (2013) called this exceptional subjective experience of the *Umwelt*, *magic environment*s. He said that this kind of phenomenon is also common in other animals, which suddenly react against invisible presences in their *Umwelt*. Many human sanctuaries possess such a special "atmosphere", which is, however, a product of the culturally mediated subjective construction of the experience.

The theory of *imaginative process as higher mental function* (Tateo, 2020) states that imaginative and non-imaginative modalities of experiencing reality are not operating in alternation (*either* one *or* the other). In the construction of the life world (*Umwelt*), human beings constantly use imaginative and non-imaginative modalities as complementary. Imagination is thus one of the higher mental functions, based on sign mediation (see Chapter 1) that feeds into non-imaginative modality, creating a surplus of meaning. The process follows the same sociogenetic principles of formation and complementarity of the other higher functions (Vygotsky, 2004). Figure 4.6 summarizes the features of imaginative processes so far discussed. The *Umwelt* is a web of semiotic relationships (Maran, 2020), and during the ontogenesis the different higher mental functions are formed as culturally regulated social

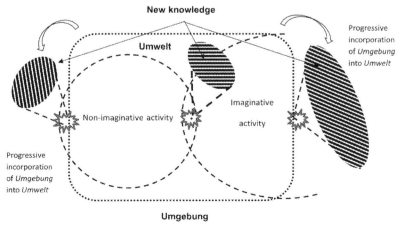

Figure 4.6 Meaning-making and imaginative/non-imaginative complementarity

interactions. In different moments of the life course, the environment presents the organism with different demands, affordances, and constraints. In the case of human beings, the environmental demands are culturally organized. As Vygotsky (2004) has already noted, children are apparently more imaginative than logical because the culture includes them in certain types of activities that afford the prevalence of one feature over another in the whole range of psychological functions.

Children do not become more "rational" as they grow up. They start to participate in formal education that requires different types of competences and values formal logic over imagination (Vygotsky, 2004). The former higher psychological functions do not disappear. The whole of the psychic organization changes according to the socio-cultural environment during the life course (Zittoun, 2006): some move to the background, and some come to the foreground, according to their socio-cultural value and to the opportunities of exerting them during social interactions.

The way human beings build and experience their *Umwelten* is the *complementary work of imaginative and non-imaginative activity, focusing on elements that go beyond the current limits of the life world* (Tateo, 2020). People make sense of their *Umwelt* through the interdependent work of higher psychic functions (i.e., thinking, imagining, remembering, feeling, and communicating). When they reach the limits of their personal bubble (see Figure 4.2), on the edge of *Umgebung*, the hierarchy of functions changes and the role of imaginative work becomes more important. Imaginative work is thus a crucial element in the emerging of novelty and in a qualitative breakthrough of the previous organization of the person/environment relationship.

The imaginative incorporation of the environment and its borders creates non-imaginative self-regulation. For instance, in the case of religious beliefs in the afterlife, signs or images (e.g., heaven or hell) regulate people's conduct in their present lives. The role of imaginative work in human development is not only to explore the unknown, but to produce the unknown as a driving force to be explored (Lapoujade, 1988).

In the theory of complementarity between imaginative and non-imaginative modes of knowing, the opposition between "real" and "imaginary" does not make sense. The meaning-making process in human experience is always a complementary work of the two modalities that feed into each other in the life world. Imagining is a higher mental function, because it is a semiotic process (see Chapter 1) that does not simply create an "alternative" to reality. It plays a fundamental role in the construction of human *Umwelt*.

THE SOCIOGENESIS OF IMAGINING

How is the imaginative process ontogenetically formed during human development? According to psychoanalysis (Freud, 1911), the infant is a self-hallucinating creature who lives their first days into a world based on the pleasure principle, where imagination is the most direct way to satisfaction. In adult life, imagination is used to satisfy personal desires, and to compensate an unsatisfactory reality: only the unsatisfied person imagines (Freud, 1911).

For Piaget (1959), imagination is the subjective assimilation of reality into the egocentric satisfaction of the individual's ego. Only at a later developmental stage, facing the inadequacy of existing cognitive structures in the understanding of the reactions of others and of the world, the child develops the capability of decentering herself from egocentric perception and accepts the existence of multiple perspectives (Kohler, 2018).

Most theories of human development have considered imagination as a by-product of the development of symbolic capability. Vygotsky believed that imagination "does not develop all at once, but very slowly and gradually evolves from more elementary and simpler forms into more complex ones" (2004, p. 12). It is assumed that imagination derives from sensorimotor schemes of exploration that develop first into imitation (Piaget, 1959), then internal persistent imitation (Baldwin, 1894), and then joint participation in social activities (Vygotsky, 2004).

However, imagination is often considered an internal and individual activity, where external influences can only provide the raw material on which imagination operates (Papastathopoulos & Kugiumutzakis, 2007). Vygotsky (2004) claimed that the relationship between the individual and the context plays a crucial role in the development of imagination:

> We have seen that imagination depends on experience, and a child's experience forms and grows gradually, and, in its profound individuality, is different from that of an adult. The child's relationship to his environment, which, through its complexity or simplicity, traditions, and influences stimulates and directs the process of creation, is very different from the adult's. The interests of the child and the adult also differ, and it is thus easy to understand why a child's imagination functions differently from an adult's.
>
> (Vygotsky, 2004, p. 31)

If imaginative processes are a higher mental function that develops sociogenetically through the progressive internalization of individual participation in collective activities, how can it also be one of the child's first modes of experiencing, and a tool for the construction of the *Umwelt*? What comes first, the imaginative capability or the experience that develops such a capability?

According to the theory that imaginative and non-imaginative modes of experiencing are complementary in the construction of the personal world, and that they both develop through progressive internalization of social interactions, it is possible to conclude that they feed into each other mutually from the very early stages of development. However, we do not know enough about the micro-genetic processes through which, day by day, persons construct their imaginative and non-imaginative ways of experiencing as epistemic tools. We must study the micro-interactions in early development during which adults prompt and suggest imaginative work to children much earlier than the symbolic play and the "as if" interactions. Moreover, we do not know how imaginative processes feed into the elaboration of non-imaginative processes. Vygotsky (2004) describes the mutual feeding of reproductive and creative imagination, resulting in a real-life object:

> The imagination's drive to be embodied, this is the real basis and motive force of creation. Every product of the imagination, stemming from reality, attempts to complete a full circle and to be embodied in reality. A product of the imagination, which has arisen in response to our drive and inspiration, shows a tendency to be embodied in real life. The imagination, by virtue of the strength of the impulses it contains, tends to become creative, that is, to actively transform whatever it has been directed at.
>
> (Vygotsky, 2004, p. 41)

During collective activities, one internalizes meanings that feed into the genesis of imaginative processes that create, in return, meanings that can be externalized and produce effects in the world. A parent presenting the child with a sentence such as "imagine that X" is producing a micro-event that leads to the internalization of different meanings of the verb "to imagine". A complete micro-genetic analysis of this process is still missing. The studies on imagining have mainly focused on the product of imaginative activity at a later age.

EDUCATING IMAGINING

Why in the end do we need to strengthen imaginative processes in children? In the market economy, knowledge is a commodity. It is subject to the principle of the creation of new needs to be satisfied by new products. Hence, the push to be creative, innovative, producing "groundbreaking" and "breathtaking" new discoveries. All the planetary problems in relation to anthropic activities (e.g., fossil fuels, climate change, migration, neoliberalist exploitation of resources) need truly innovative and utopian solutions (Bird et al., 2016). Human beings are instead stuck in the repetition of old solutions and acquired habits that inform both everyday conducts and global policies. Like language and the other higher mental functions, imagining is historically situated (Tateo, 2015; Zittoun & Gillespie, 2015) but not necessarily incremental or progressive. One cannot say that imagining in the past was *less developed* than today, as much as one cannot say that one language is *less developed* than another. So, can we *teach* imagination to children, hoping for their capability of designing a better future? The answer is naturally negative. If imaginative processes are higher mental functions like language, problem solving, reflection, they cannot be *transmitted* but can be *educated*. A pedagogy of imagination must be based on:

- its historical and cultural forms;
- its ontogenesis and sociogenesis;
- its culturally situated practices and tools in knowledge building (e.g., imagination in science);
- its relation with other higher mental functions (e.g. memory, reflection, problem solving, etc.) and with non-imaginative processes;
- its cognitive, affective, and ethical dimensions.

Philosophy began with surprise. Imagination leads beyond the surprise towards the *intentional production of surprise* (Lapoujade, 1988), based on abductive forms of inference. The epistemic value of the imaginative process is exactly the potentiality for exploring new portions of the *Umwelt* that have not yet been empirically reached. That's why imagination is often the first target of authoritarians, consumerism, and orthodoxy. Hegemony needs to rely on solid belief about the best of all possible worlds, on the reproductive imagination of advertisement and propaganda. Any attempt to intentionally produce alternative worlds, to use the generative and productive imagination, to play the "as if" games (Vaihinger, 2014), is monitored with suspicious anxiety.

IMAGINING AS A HIGHER MENTAL FUNCTION

One can consider imaginative and non-imaginative modalities as a complementary pair. We can use the metaphor of the shoreline to clarify the concept: a shoreline on the beach is a continuous pendulum-like shift between water and land. Water and land alternate rhythmically, forming a whole. Sometimes, a portion of the space is occupied by the sand and the next moment it is covered by water. However, remove either the water or the sand and it will no longer be a shore. One can think about imaginative processes in a similar way: two complementary modes of experience – imaginative and non-imaginative – that are both always present and continuously dancing in our life world. Sometimes, the solid ground of imagination provides stability and continuity to our experiencing, like in the perennial immutability of myth and social imaginary. Other times, the rippling waters of non-imaginative process cast doubts on our perceived world. The safe shore of taken-for-granted beliefs sometimes detracts our thoughts away from the deep waters, which hide sea monsters and sirens of unconscious imaginary. In any case, imaginative and non-imaginative mental life cannot be separated because they feed into each other like the sea and the shore in the rhythm of tides.

Reflection:

The term "psychodiversity" has been used for the past 25 years with different meanings. First, it was used to describe how different persons have different motivations for action. Nowadays, it is used as a synonym for "neurodiversity", meaning that persons who function in a different way do not necessarily have a "disorder". Those people find their own developmental trajectory that is not "normative". Finally, the term "psychodiversity" can mean that psychological processes develop in a specific and unique socio-cultural context. In this sense, every psychology is "indigenous psychology" (Marsella, 2013). In the latter sense, psychodiversity is used in the same way as "biodiversity".

The complementarity between imaginative and non-imaginative modalities raises further questions: to what extent is the process of imagining related to the processes of knowing and understanding? If one accepts a reproductive idea of imagination, this suggests that one can imagine only by recombining what one already knows. If one adopts a productive or generative idea of imagination, like Vygotsky's (2004) proposed, then one can only know what one can imagine. So, how does one reach the shoreline? By coming from the beach or by coming from the sea?

Of course, such a question does not make sense, because the shoreline is an in-between space, a point of encounter that emerges from the complementarity of its elements. In the same way, the process of knowing – forming a well-founded belief – and the process of understanding – being aware of the genesis and the conditions of the belief – are formed through the complementary contribution of imaginative and non-imaginative processes that feed into each other.

Historically, human societies have developed different forms of knowledge production and different forms of understanding. It is thus possible to argue that there can be different forms of imagining (Pieterse & Parekh, 1995). The rationalistic Western perspective has used imagination as a negative attribute to downgrade different cultures. For instance, indigenous epistemologies have claimed different relationships between imaginative and non-imaginative modes of experiencing than the Western conception. They have often been considered "primitive" for that. The Western concept of consciousness was based on the idea of being present to oneself in a non-imaginative way. Yet, how can one have access to oneself without imaginative work? If we don't acknowledge and respect the *psychodiversity* within ourselves, how can we honor that of the other cultures?

Talking of imagination as a product has only led to the multiplication of definitions and to an empty signifier (imagination) that can be filled with any possible theoretical nuance (Sepper, 2013). In cultural psychology, imagination is understood as a higher mental function among the others (Figure 4.7).

If one considers the psychic life as a whole system to which the different mental functions contribute, assuming qualitatively different configurations in the course of human sociogenetic development, one can work out reasonable theoretical orientations. In Figure 4.7, I present some examples, of course not all-encompassing, of how imagining is related to the other functions in different moments of life. In an earlier moment of the life course, when higher mental functions are characterized by progressive sociogenesis, and experiences appear for the first time, sensorimotor activities, persistent meaningful selective imitation, and vicarious experiences prevail over the systematic and schematic organization of the world. In this period, one can guess how the mental functions that support that way of experiencing will be hierarchically more relevant than, for instance, those that support the schematization of the world. At a later phase of development, such as for instance after entering formal education, social life requires different forms of interaction with the world. Formal logic and social skills based on cognitive flexibility and a memory based on the management of a large amount of information will prevail hierarchically.

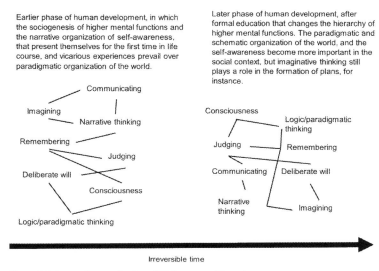

Figure 4.7 Systemic organization of higher mental functions

In both phases of the life course, all functions work together as a system, but their relative hierarchical role in the whole system changes. We know from Vygotsky (2004) that imaginative processes are not stronger during early childhood, because they also depend on the way one organizes and accumulates experience. So, children are not *more* imaginative than adults. The systemic organization of higher mental functions in relation to the social demands at that age are simply qualitatively different from those of an adult. At any age, human beings live on the shoreline where imaginative and non-imaginative modes of experiencing work together to form our life worlds. A unified theory of imagining can help us to recognize the different configurations of imaginative and non-imaginative modes in the different contexts of human activity and to appreciate this special form in which human beings make sense of their world.

SUMMARY OF CHAPTER 4

In Chapter 4, we have discussed the importance of imagination in everyday life and in science. We have shown how imagining is related to knowing and then presented two main theories of imagination in cultural psychology: the theory of imagination as uncoupling, and the theory of imagination as a higher mental function. Both theories understand imagination as a fundamental feature of the human psyche that develops in the context of culturally organized activities. Finally, we have discussed the sociogenesis of imagination and the possibility of educating to imagination.

Check your knowledge and reflect

Task: Can you think about an everyday activity that involves imaginative and non-imaginative modalities? How do the different psychological functions concur in the activity? Who are the persons involved? What are the cultural forms, metaphors, images, rituals implied? Write a short essay (maximum two pages) elaborating your personal view and using the concepts presented so far. Then, share your essay with two colleagues and ask for their feedback.

NOTES

1. Abduction is a particular form of inference, "Since Peirce's theorization, scientific knowledge creation is understood as a triadic process of hypothesizing, modeling, and proving [...] Each step is characterized by a leading inferential structure, namely abduction to speculate on new hypotheses, deduction to draw the possible consequences and relationship and induction to prove the hypothesis. A theory can be said to be established when the knowledge achieves a character of generalization" (Tateo, 2015, p. 48).
2. The term comes from the verb "geben" (to give) and the prefix "um". It literally means what is "given", outside the borders of the actively constructed world of the individual. It is what escapes the person, and at the same time what is there not because of the person. According to von Uexküll (2013), the surroundings are the opposite of the optimal Umwelt of the organism.

REFERENCES

Baldwin, J. M. (1894). Imitation: A chapter in the natural history of consciousness. *Mind, 3*(9), 26–55.

Bird, F., Twiss, S. B., Pedersen, K. P., Miller, C. A., & Grelle, B. (Eds.). (2016). *Practices of global ethics: Historical backgrounds, current issues, and future prospects.* Edinburgh: Edinburgh University Press.

Capon, R. F. (2002). *The supper of the lamb: A culinary entertainment.* New York: Modern Library.

Cropper, W. H. (2001). *Great physicists: The life and times of leading physicists from Galileo to Hawking.* New York: Oxford University Press.

Dario, N., & Tateo, L. (Eds.). (2022). *New perspectives on mind-wandering.* Cham: Springer.

Freud, S. (1911). Formulations on the two principles of mental functioning. Yearbook, 3 (1). In Standard Edition of *Freud's Psychological Writings, 12,* pp. 215–226.

Heisig, J. W. (1976). Jung and the "imago dei": The future of an idea. *The Journal of Religion, 56*(1), 88–104.

Johnson, M. (2013). *The body in the mind: The bodily basis of meaning, imagination, and reason.* Chicago, IL: University of Chicago Press.

Jung, C. G. (1959). The archetypes and collective unconscious. In *The collected works of C. G. Jung,* trans. R. F. C. Hull, Bollingen Series XX. Princeton, NJ: Princeton University Press.

Kohler, A. (2018). From the logic of the child to a natural logic: Perspectives as knowledge. *Human Arenas, 1*(1), 97–111.

Lapoujade, M. N. (1988). *Filosofía de la imaginación.* Cerro del agua, Mexico: Siglo XXI.

Maran, T. (2020). *Ecosemiotics: The study of signs in changing ecologies.* Cambridge: Cambridge University Press.

Marsella, A. J. (2013). All psychologies are indigenous psychologies: Reflections on psychology in a global era. *Psychology International, 24*(4), 5–7.

McAllister, J. W. (2012). Thought experiment and the exercise of imagination in science. In M. Frappier, L. Meynell, & J. R. Brown (Eds.), *Thought experiments in philosophy, science, and the arts* (pp. 11–29). London: Routledge.

Miščević, N. (2012). Political thought experiments from Plato to Rawls. In M. Frappier, L. Meynell, & J. R. Brown (Eds.), *Thought experiments in philosophy, science, and the arts* (pp. 191–206). London: Routledge.

Norton, J. D. (2012). Chasing the light. Einstein's most famous thought experiment. In M. Frappier, L. Meynell, & J. R. Brown (Eds.), *Thought experiments in philosophy, science, and the arts* (pp. 123–140). London: Routledge.

Papastathopoulos, S., & Kugiumutzakis, G. (2007). The intersubjectivity of imagination: The special case of imaginary companions. In S. Bråten (Ed.), *On being moved: From mirror neurons to empathy* (pp. 219–233). Amsterdam: John Benjamins.

Piaget, J. (1959). *The language and thought of the child*. London: Routledge.

Pieterse, J. N., & Parekh, B. C. (eds.) (1995). *The decolonization of imagination: Culture, knowledge and power*. London: Zed Books.

Sepper, D. L. (2013). *Understanding imagination*. Dordrecht: Springer.

Shepard, R. N. (1987). Toward a universal law of generalization for psychological science. *Science, 237*, 1317–1323. https://doi.org/10.1126/science.3629243

Tateo, L. (2015). The nature of generalization in psychology. In G. Marsico, R. Andrisano Ruggieri, & S. Salvatore (Eds.), *Reflexivity and psychology* (pp. 45–64). Charlotte, NC: Information Age Publishing.

Tateo, L. (2017). Poetic destroyers. Vico, Emerson and the aesthetic dimension of experiencing. *Culture & Psychology, 23*(3), 337–355.

Tateo, L. (2019). The cultures of grief: The practice of post-mortem photography and iconic internalized voices. *Human Affairs, 28*(4), 471–482.

Tateo, L. (2020). *A theory of imagining, knowing, and understanding*. Cham: Springer Nature.

Tateo, L. (2023). Fear. In V. Glaveanu (Ed.), *Creativity: A new vocabulary* (pp. 87–97). Cham: Springer International Publishing.

von Uexküll, J. (2013). *A foray into the worlds of animals and humans: With a theory of meaning*. Minneapolis, MN: University of Minnesota Press.

Vaihinger, H. (2014). *The philosophy of as if*. London: Routledge.

Vygotsky, L. S. (2004). Imagination and creativity in childhood. *Journal of Russian and East European Psychology, 42*(1), 7–97.

White, M., & Gribbin, J. (2002). *Stephen Hawking: A life in science*. Washington, D.C.: Joseph Henry Press.

Zittoun, T. (2006). *Transitions: Development through symbolic resources*. Greenwich (CT): InfoAge.

Zittoun, T., & Gillespie, A. (2015). *Imagination in human and cultural development*. London: Routledge.

CHAPTER 5 # Borders

Scan the QR-code to access additional materials and watch outstanding international scholars discussing key concepts.

LEARNING GOALS

1. To acquire the basic concepts of the bordering process
2. To understand the role of borders in psyche and society
3. To learn the general genetic law of bordering development

CHAPTER OVERVIEW

In this chapter, the bordering process and the concept of borders and border crossing will be presented. The construction, crossing, and demolition of borders is a fundamental way of organizing both psychic experience and the environment. The border is a constitutive part of the triadic fundamental unit of analysis in co-genetic logic. We will discuss the phenomenology of borders, their semiotic functioning and the consequences of human psychological experience. Finally, we will present the general genetic law of bordering development and its role in psychological functioning.

GROUP ACTIVITY FOR INSTRUCTOR: BORDERS

The class is divided into small groups (3–5 students) and the task is to walk around the site (campus, school, etc.) and try to identify *visible and invisible* kinds of borders. The instructions are:

1. Walk around the site and identify *visible and invisible* kinds of borders, stop for a few minutes on a border
2. take pictures and draw a map of the place you have selected
3. Mark on the map all the borders you can discover
4. Discuss the experience with your group.

After the experience, the instructor leads a plenary discussion to analyze the experience, focusing in particular on:

- what is the given structure ("border as it seems to be")?
- what is the given function ("border as it seems to work")?
- how can you describe the possibilities of direct modification of the present border? (Maximum movability of this border as it currently is)
- what kind of sign-mediated actions is it possible to accomplish?

Reflection questions

The activity is aimed at activating the students' attention to the borders in the environment, involving both embodiment and observation.

- What were your feelings on the borders?
- What signs did you find on the borders?
- There were different kinds of borders? Why?
- Was there a duration of borders?
- Did you find any relation to other concepts of cultural psychology?

BORDERS AND BORDERING IN THE ENVIRONMENT AND IN THE MIND[1]

If one looks at the person in Figure 5.1, one can see how she sits in the Oslo metro in such a way as to occupy the space of three seats. Every other person would recognize the message and avoid sitting in the (apparently) free seats on the left of the girl. In other words, the girl has settled an area around her that is forbidden to others. She set borders around what she appropriated as her "personal space". Why so? Besides, how is it possible that other people can interpret her message in the same way, and not simply ignore the material (the bag on the seat) and immaterial (the close body posture and the extended legs, the choice to take the middle seat, etc.) signs?

The use of indexical signs (landmarks, scent, etc.) to delimit a territory is typical of many species (Eason, Cobbs & Trinca, 1999), including humans. Many episodes in human history, including for instance the foundation of Ancient Rome by Romulus, involve borders. Romulus and Remus were the twin sons of the god Mars and the vestal Rea Silvia, a priestess and king's daughter (Cornell, 1975). On the king's orders, the illegitimate new-born were cast into the river Tiber. The children survived and were found by a she-wolf who suckled them in her cave called *Lupercal*. Rescued by shepherds, the now-adult twins took revenge and killed the king. They decided to build a new town where the city of Rome will later sit. Having interpreted the auguries in his favour, Romulus started digging a trench with a plow to mark the limits of the new city (Figure 5.2). His brother Remus, who believed he

Figure 5.1 Bordering of personal space (Photo by Tateo, 2023)

Figure 5.2 Bartolomeo Pinelli, Romulus marks out a line around the Palatine Hill (1818), Thorvaldsen Museum, Copenhagen (Photo by Jakob Faurvig, Public Domain).

was the legitimate one to rule the town, jumped over the trench to challenge his brother, who killed him in the fight.

The myth describes an initial whole (the twins, a virgin territory) on which a distinction (the trench) is produced (see Chapter 1). Thus, two parts are created (the trace of the future town and its surroundings) together with a relationship of value between the parts of the whole (inside–outside the town, the different status of the twins). The trench is a border that implies a regulation (conditions for crossing) and the potentiality of violating it (Remus's crossing is a challenge to authority). A former undivided space becomes an appropriated territory and acquires the identity of a nascent town (Lambert, 2015), surrounded by its "outside". Now, the contested territories and borders are a prevalent source of conflicts and tragedies.

Nevertheless, human beings also seem to create boundaries when they inhabit temporary spaces (such as the metro in Figure 5.1) or around themselves. Unlike territorial animals, they seem to attach a "personal" meaning to the establishment of boundaries. According to Scott (1993): "Personal space boundaries (PSB) form dynamic lines of demarcation between an individual's internal (body, mind, and spirit) and external environments. Boundaries vary in permeability and flexibility" (Scott, 1993, p. 12).

Borders are ubiquitous: bordering in human activities can be experienced in different modalities. Border zones have peculiar qualities (Brambilla,

2015) – they can be physical barriers or passages; sound-scapes; smell-scapes; surfaces; visual cues or barriers to the gaze (Tateo & Marsico, 2022). They can be ethical modalities such as law-scapes (see Ansaloni & Tedeschi, 2016; Philippopoulos-Mihalopoulos, 2013). For instance, any urban space is composed of different zones with slightly different sets of rules. Those zones are marked by multiple types of signs that suggest normative behaviors (Tateo & Marsico, 2022), such as street signals, surveillance cameras, but also architectural features such as benches in public spaces that do not allow sleeping on them to keep away the homeless.

The common feature is that they work as internalized semiotic artifacts that regulate psychic life (Tateo & Marsico, 2021). "Man's position in the world is defined by the fact that in every dimension of his being and behavior he finds himself at every moment between two boundaries" – humans live in between a "more or less, a right and left; an above or below, a better or worse" (Simmel, 1918/2010, p. 1).

Georg Simmel (1858–1918) was a German sociologist and philosopher. He made a unique synthesis between phenomenological, structuralist, and cultural analysis.

CULTURAL PSYCHOLOGY OF BORDERS

The field of border studies in cultural psychology has been established by Pina Marsico (2011; 2016; Marsico et al., 2013). Starting from the interest of the whole/parts relationships (Marsico & Varzi, 2016), she noted how borders are abundant and ubiquitous in human life, and yet elusive when one tries to grasp their essence. Borders are usually understood as natural or artificial boundaries that delimit a territory or a state, or anything that separates something from the adjacent surroundings. Yet, borders also unite at the same time, much as a locked door in a corridor that has a "Welcome" floormat on the outside.

On deeper inspection, one can see how many objects and events can be considered borders. Whether material or immaterial; concrete or imaginary; well-defined or vague; more or less permeable – borders define what is admitted or not into a bounded space: the friendly, the useful, the alien, or the dangerous element. Such a daily phenomenon is of course of interest for cultural psychology. According to co-genetic logic, borders are co-constitutive parts of any living system (see Chapter 1), including the human psyche.

William James (1842–1910) was an American pragmatist and radical empiricist philosopher and psychologist. He studied consciousness, spiritual life, emotions, and free will. He is considered the "Father of American psychology".

BORDERS AND MIND

According to William James (1950), the primary operation of psychic life is the emergence of consciousness from the segmentation and stabilization of a stream of thought into units (James, 1950). Thus, no conscious psychic life can emerge without operating a distinction (see Chapter 1). However, operating a distinction does not create unrelated entities but generates a dynamic system. Every distinction implies a higher-level of organization and at the same time every bind creates distinctiveness.

> By choosing two items from the undisturbed store of natural things
> in order to designate them as 'separate', we have already related them
> to one another in our consciousness, we have emphasized these two
> together against whatever lies between them. And conversely, we can
> only sense those things to be related which we have previously somehow
> isolated from one another; things must first be separated from one
> another in order to be together.
>
> (Simmel, 1994, p. 5)

When one distinguishes elements of a continuous flow, the new sub-parts acquire different values. Similarly, when one binds elements that were previously perceived as distinct, this produces an internal hierarchy in the new whole. In the example of Romulus and Remus, the border-sign (the trench) immediately produces a distinction with some co-genetic features: the border, an inside, and an outside with different values attached to each part. The distinction of sub-parts can produce value difference ("X is different from Y, so one must be better than the other"), or value can be added to produce a differentiation ("X is better than Y, so they must be somehow different") (Valsiner, 2001). Figure and background, inside and outside, central and peripheral co-define each other's properties and values in function of their relationship to a third organism:

> as I am apprehending an A, I also apprehend a non-A in some sense. So
> we have to do with a difference regarding what is apprehended [. . .]
> a difference regarding what stands opposite [*gegenübersteht*] each
> intellectual experience as its object [*Gegenstand*] [. . .]. In the non-A,
> then, there is a further objective factor, the 'non,' as it were, supervening
> on the A.
>
> (Meinong 1983, pp. 14–15)

Alexius Meinong (1853–1920) was an Austrian philosopher, known for his unique ontology of objects, his philosophy of mind, and theory of value.

As we have seen in Chapter 1, by removing the boundary, a distinction between inside and outside is no longer possible. The operation of distinction produces an "inclusive separation" (Valsiner, 2001), a higher-order level of organization in which the distinction makes sense.

Hence, the fundamental role of borders with reference to the development of consciousness:

> the Consciousness is speech for oneself, it originates in society with
> language [. . .] Speech is always a dialogue [. . .] Consciousness is
> a dialogue with oneself. Already the fact that the child first listens
> and understands and then acquires verbal consciousness points out
> that: (1) Consciousness develops from experience; (2) Speaking with
> himself = consciously acting, the child takes the position of the other,
> relates to himself as to another person, imitates another person speaking

to him, replaces the other person in relation to himself, learns to be another person in relation to his proper body. Consciousness is a double.
(Zavershneva & van der Veer, 2018, p. 75)

Borders are also strictly related to identity. Dwelling on one of the sides of a border provides a particular identity status (e.g., citizenship). The act of crossing a border also changes one's identity (from being a citizen, one becomes a migrant). This is also true for temporal borders, as for instance the achievement of the "legal age" for a young person in different cultures.

BORDERS AND SIGNS

If borders acquire meanings in relation to someone who is oriented towards them, in order for a bordering process to function an *interpretant* is required for whom the borders are meaningful. Borders cannot exist without an act of *interpretation*. Thus, bordering is an act of semiosis (see Chapter 1).

The emerge of any distinction (drawing a border) immediately creates a triad ("A">"non-A">border) as a higher-level co-genetic system, in which the sub-parts are co-defined by their relationships (Marsico & Varzi, 2016). For instance, when we talk about "our people" or "low income groups" we immediately create a boundary with those who are "not our people" or "non low income groups".

As in semiosis, the elements of the triad establish several relations (Picione, 2021; Picione et al., 2022) (see Chapter 1), such as:

a) substitution, because the border by definition bounds its object;
b) distinction, because by definition the border is between two different entities;
c) unification, because the emergence of a border creates a triadic higher-level system of elements that were not necessarily sub-parts of the triad before; and
d) temporality, because this mutual relationship genetically leads to the emergence of further phenomena.

The production of the distinction is accompanied by the operation of adding different *values* to the sub-parts (Marsico et al., 2013). So, once alternatives are created, one *must* be better than the other. This operation is necessary to allow the establishment of a hierarchy of both social power and personal preference.

The bordering also establishes a double negation, in which "A" is defined as something that is also "non-non-A". The same distinction creates the permeability conditions under which "non-A" can become quasi-A in some respect. The co-definition of "A" through "non-A" is bidirectional. For instance, values such as "masculinity" or "patriotism" ("A") in a given historical moment are defined by a set of positive properties and by a complementary set of "non-masculinity" or "non-patriotism" (non-A).

The border between the two fields of meaning is marked by signs such as actions, symbols, outfits, artifacts, etc. Thus, a *real* male or a *real* patriot is someone who does *masculine* or *patriotic* stuff, who dresses or talks like a "man" or a "patriot". At the same time, "A" is also the one who refrains doing feminine or antipatriotic stuff (not-non-A). The field of "non-masculine" or "non-patriotic", in return, includes an infinite number of instances that vary in magnitude from the "feminine" to the "quasi-masculine", from the "gay" to the "non-masculine", etc. (see Figure 1.3 in Chapter 1).

In the border zone, we can find several actions and signs that in the course of time and in different cultural contexts can move from one field of meaning to the other (e.g., beauty treatments, tattoos, accessories, flags, foods, etc.).

A certain degree of uncertainty implied in the non-A field allows development, for it opens to the possibility of misunderstanding, misinterpretation, negotiation, and even deceiving. This leads to new possibilities of meaning-making. Any action of border crossing is changing the system whilst establishing a new distinction at the same time, requiring new interpretation. Any action upon the body can for instance represent a sign whose meaning is determined by the complementarity between its being (more or less) "masculine", "non-masculine", "almost feminine", "totally feminine", etc.

THE DEVELOPMENTAL FUNCTION OF BORDERS: THE CONCEPT OF *GEGENSTAND*

Borders play a very important developmental function. Something becomes a border when a living agent becomes interested in it. A closed door can be just a piece of furniture, and it does not become a border unless the person decides to exit the room. One can be surrounded by many things without interacting with them but once attention and intention are directed towards those things, they become objects, they acquire meaning. "The crucial role in this transformation is the role of the agent: by acting upon things in nature, these become objects. These objects can resist our actions (stand against us = Gegen+stand), or can evade us" (Valsiner, 2014, p. 153).

Gegenstanden (in German) do not exist in themselves – they populate our lives: we miss, love, or hate them. They exist as parts of the meaning-making processes. Whereas a *Gegenstand* is a person, a pet, a material (or immaterial) object, the agent establishes a relationship in which directionality and resistance are complementary phenomena: they appear as soon as an orientation emerges (Figure 5.3).

During ontogenesis, human beings are repeatedly confronted with extrinsic or intrinsic developmental tasks (Havighurst, 1948). On the one hand, children very early in life become curious about the surrounding environment, and challenge themselves to overcome small obstacles, grasp objects

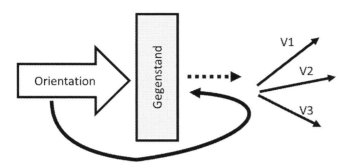

Figure 5.3 The dynamics of directionality/resistance (adapted from Valsiner, 2014a, p. 154)

out of their reach, cross self-imposed limits. On the other hand, children's development is socially guided through a set of steps and goals that should occur at the "right" time. A toilet in the home bathroom may be not particularly interesting for an infant, until the parents do not make it salient by establishing that toilet training is a proper developmental task to be achieved within the first 18–24 months.

The dialectics between orientation, resistance, and overcoming, which crystallizes around objects, become *Gegenstanden*, a fundamental motor of development. Borders are the necessary forms through which human development unfolds its path, which is at the same time unique (everyone is different) and socially guided (more or less "socially acceptable" paths) (see Chapter 3). Developmental outcomes are not completely predicable and vectorial (vectors V1, V2, and V3 in Figure 5.3) as they result from the complex dialectics between orientation, resistance, motivation, and feedback (Chaudhary et al., 2017).

The concept of *Gegenstand* as a more or less permeable border helps to better understand Vygotsky's idea that "instruction and development do not proceed in parallel" (Zavershneva & van der Veer, 2018, p. 314). Indeed, he distinguished between "three things: the level, the paths, the zone" (Zavershneva & van der Veer, 2018, p. 314). In Figure 5.3, one can see how the "orientation" emerges from an actual level of development, which sets the condition for the person to encounter something that becomes a *Gegenstand*. For instance, a child may be confronted with a new problem "X" – encountered for intrinsic or extrinsic reasons – that must be solved. If the problem falls within the actual level of development, it will not represent a border (dotted line in Figure 5.3) and will be totally permeable to crossing. However, this is a rare situation of a very boring object.

If one understands resistance as complementary to orientation (as both parts of the meaningful relationship with the world), there cannot be a completely permeable object of experience. In this case, what becomes important is the *path* through which the border "X" will be overcome. The *dance* of

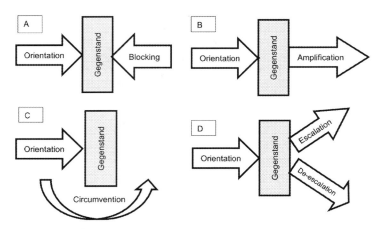

Figure 5.4 Examples of different paths of orientation/resistance

resistance and orientation can produce different paths leading to processes of opposition, deviation, amplification, scaffolding, etc. through selective inhibition/promotion (Figure 5.4).

The different paths share the characteristic of being part of a developmental process. Although they do not necessarily lead to a positive or incremental outcome, they are always future-oriented. The person can let go of immediate gratification in the interest of later goals (Figure 5.4A); can circumvent or simply ignore the problem (Figure 5.4C); some children can simply run away or be silent, while others can speak up (Figure 5.4B and 5.4D). The adults can interpret children's paths to find a way out in different ways. Circumvention or escalation can be interpreted as "challenging behavior". De-escalation or indifference can be interpreted as obedience or shyness. Amplification can be interpreted as opposition or rebellion.

According to Vygotsky, "instruction and development do not coincide. They are two different processes with very complex interrelationships. Instruction is only useful when it moves ahead of development" (Vygotsky, 1987, p. 212).

Thus, instruction fosters development when it becomes a *Gegenstand* that generates various possible paths in the same new formation (vectors in Figure 5.4).

> When it does, it impels or awakens a whole series of functions that are in a stage of maturation lying in the zone of proximal development. [. . .] Instruction would be completely unnecessary if it merely utilized what had already matured in the developmental process, if it were not itself a source of development.
>
> (Vygotsky, 1987, p. 212)

SELECTIVE INTERNALIZATION OF BORDERS

In semiotic cultural psychology, psychic life is a process of purposeful production and interpretation of signs, through cycles of culturally guided and selective internalization and externalization. Borders are not just something "out there". As discussed earlier, they emerge in the purposeful orientation of the person during future-oriented action in everyday life.

Signs regulate both one's own and others' feelings and conducts (Valsiner, 2014), and they are disseminated in the human-featured environment as street signs, architectural elements, sounds, etc. Personal self-regulating meanings and overcoming the different paths to *Gegenstand* allow for instance a person to ignore an expectation or a norm (or to expect others to know about it), or not use one oneself. If one encounters a regulatory sign in the environment, whose limited meaning is internalized (e.g., "Smoke can kill"), one produces the socially correct interpretant (e.g., "I shall not smoke") (Figure 5.5).

However, as interpretation is purposeful and all signs are ambivalent and polysemic, the first interpretant can become the object of a new semiotic act. So, one can produce a further sign, a new regulation ("'I will smoke anyway"), that overcomes and neutralizes the first interpretant, while both are still working (Figure 5.4). This is the most basic process upon which distinction-making emerges ("I am me, and you are you, and *we are different*"). Through hierarchical regulation of signs *over* other signs, distinctions and values can be demolished or circumnavigated to create new meanings (e.g., "I am me, but I do not care, so I will do that *anyway*") that can lead to different externalizations. According to Marsico *et al.* (2013), meaning-making, distinction-making, and value-adding are exactly the three processes for construction of borders in minds and in society.

In the person's life course, the environment progressively populates with meaningful objects and persons that constitute a complex system of (internal

Figure 5.5 Ambivalent border sign (photo by Tateo, 2018)

and external) identities and boundaries. Such a complex system multiplies hierarchies and value differences, generating diverse configurations of vectorial forces (Figure 5.5). On the one hand, distinction-making therefore unifies the parts into a system of meaningful relations (substitution, distinction, unification, and temporality) based on certain criteria. On the other hand, borders reduce ambiguity through the act of demarcation, by limiting the space and the expected behavior; while, since the division is neither rigid nor fixed, the interpretation of the border/sign as a space for fluidity between both sides appears, and the ambiguity re-emerges (Marsico et al., 2013). This space for fluidity favors the conception of the border as a "space in between" that

> is neither a cuttable and divisible presence into discrete and tangible things, nor a mere 'nothing' cuttable off our conceptualization, but it's a ground (for a figure) in which flow and counter-flow is a fluid interplay amid distinct bounded context takes place.
> (Marsico, 2011, p. 191)

Ambiguity remains a fundamental aspect of borders (see Chapter 6), as well as polysemy being an important feature of signs (Figure 5.6). The

Figure 5.6 Border ambiguity when forbidden swimming is allowed. The sign on top says "swimming forbidden for absence of bay-watcher", the sign on the bottom says "swimming allowed" (photo by Tateo, 2016)

inherent ambivalence of the border creates a space for negotiation and dialogue, but is also where misunderstanding and possible confusion may arise. It allows the coexistence of different parts in a dialogue within the same whole (Marsico, 2016) and the emergence of a multiplicity of symbolic and material interactions (Brambilla, 2015). The space in-between provides a richness of meaning and symbolic interactions, which require negotiation and dialogue between the parts.

The meaning of the border becomes salient and significant when it is meaningful to *someone*. For instance, when someone wants to cross the border, the latter shows both its coercive power and the possibility of its circumnavigation. Border zones are at the same time places of control and places of multiplication of more or less legal activities and trades. The human being is the "bordering creature that has no border" (Simmel 1994, p. 10); establishing distinctions is also opening connections and any crossing is also a new bordering (Marsico 2011; Tateo 2016).

THE GENERAL GENETIC LAW OF BORDERING DEVELOPMENT

The concept of the border is very important to understand developmental processes such as the constitution of the Self, the I–other relationships, the categorization of experiences (see Chapter 1), and the differentiation of psychic systems (Marsico & Tateo, 2017). The border is an element of transition that simultaneously unites and divides two parts, accounting for the developmental dialectics between identity and alterity; continuity and discontinuity; conflict and negotiation; innovation and reproduction; *Gegenstand* and transcendence; the relationship between paths and zones; acceptable and non-acceptable paths of development; etc.

The concept of emerging borders becomes fundamental in studying human psychological functioning and the genesis of meaning. As a result of this genesis, a phenomenon and its complement are identified by a person as "X" *and* "non-X" (e.g., "I am X and not Y"; "X is fair and Y is unfair"; "inside "X" is my home and behind the door "Y" is not my home"; etc.). Meaning exists as a system in psychic experience: X has a relation of distinction, substitution, unification, and temporality with non-X.

To have a regulatory function, borders must appear at intra-psychological levels following a *general genetic law of bordering development*:[2] borders first appear at inter-psychological level (in social interactions, as artifacts, as environmental affordances, etc.), and then they appear again at the intra-psychological level as regulatory signs (Tateo & Marsico, 2021) (Figure 5.7).

The border is a sign that immediately creates a triadic system (A>non-A>border), in which a differential value is attached to the distinction-making ("A" MUST be better than "non-A"). Later, the sign is internalized and regulates the psychological functioning, in relation to meaning-making in

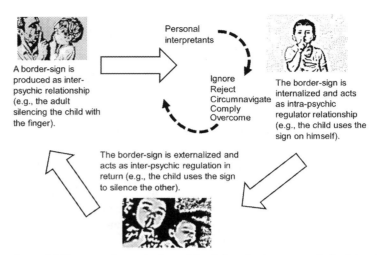

Figure 5.7 The general genetic law of bordering development and the internalization/externalization cycle

relation to the self (leading to different possible interpretants depending on the individual purpose), the Others, and the environment (through externalized signs).

One can conceive of ontogenetic development as a continuous production, maintenance, and demolition of border-signs, operating in both the extra-psychological and the intra-psychological world. In the external or physical world, borders are about modifying the environment and space–time in which humans live. In the internal experience of the world, borders regulate the feelings, sense of intimacy, and the definition/modification/negotiation of identities. The very moment the border is defined, it mediates the person's relationship with the environment, creating a distinction in the field and in the flow of events, shaping the conducts. The relationship is inherently asymmetric to the extent that the two sides of the border do not have the same value for the person or group. Value depends on the agent's orientation, which leads to a certain degree of preference or value charging of one sub-part compared to the other.

Social guidance of development works by creating meaningful temporal borders (Vygotsky, 1998), as for instance the sub-segmentation of life course into the invention of adolescence, post-adolescence, young adulthood, fourth-age, etc. Each culture suggests a different segmentation and timing according to folk theories of development. Nevertheless, as an act of signification bordering creates a *differential* (an asymmetry of magnitude in the value of the two sides) that colors affectively human lifelong development. Suffice to think about adolescence and its affective colorations: "othering" (us and them); nostalgia (for the other side); secrecy (what is visible and invisible); envy (the fruit in the neighbour's garden); etc.

Different meanings and values are produced along the inward/outward axis as the existence of the border creates an asymmetry between what is inside and what is outside. On the one hand, the border acquires its meaning from the people: a line may become a border depending on the people's purpose, actions, and intentions. Borders emerge, unfold, develop, and disappear over time. The double movement of internalization/externalization between borders in space and borders in the mind creates a number of incongruities and connections. The border is thus a developmental *locus* in living open systems (Marsico, 2016). It is a place of both tension and pacification; meeting and potential clash; discrimination and desire; violence and dialogue. It marks and puts into relationship what is possible to know, to say or to do with what is unknowable, unspeakable, or unworkable. It defines what is crossable and what is not even approachable, dividing order on one side and chaos on the other, but showing people the possibility of crossing.

Learning to recognize borders in the social environment is an important developmental task for children, whose formal education often leads to spending hours trying to learn how to color within the lines. The developing person is expected to internalize the dynamics of borders for her own identity in relation to others. Learning what is allowed and what is forbidden at a specific age is a milestone of moral development in all civilizations. Take for instance, a two-year-old child who finds it irresistible to climb staircases at home, which clearly affords climbing! Her parents constantly keep an eye on the infant with concern, ready to utter lovingly: "don't do that, it's dangerous!". The staircase thus become a *border* for the child, as soon as a particular sign ("don't do that") is repeatedly associated with it producing a new meaning-complex. Besides, the staircase would not be a meaningful border without the kid's purposeful action of trying to climb it. The border would not be effective either unless the child internalized the sign and used it to regulate her own conduct. Moreover, the *value* of the staircase changes as a consequence of the bordering: it can become even *more* attractive to climb, exactly because it is forbidden.

Interpreting the border-sign, the child can choose different paths (Figure 5.4). She can comply with the interdiction, reject it, ignore it, or simply produce a new sign that overcomes the previous one ("I know it is forbidden but I will climb anyway"). This very basic process of border internalization that creates a differential and a system of Self-regulation is not limited to childhood, and it works along the life course. Humans constantly strive to cross both self and hetero-produced borders, as can be observed in many mundane phenomena, from marketing to sports performances. The meaning of

> actions, places and events can be escalated–deescalated through processes of semiotic regulation of access to those objects. The most common form of symbolic regulation of access is any kind of ticketing [. . .] Establishing the price of an access and providing symbolic tools to

mark it (tickets, bracelets, etc.) immediately can turn a quite ordinary holiday or concert, into an extraordinary experience.

(Tateo & Marsico, 2019, p. xxiv)

A border or a prohibition produces a differential between the two parts of a system (e.g., inside/outside the "priority boarding" queue, the "economy comfort" class, or the "VIP" zone), especially alluring to customers as it becomes an identity marker.

SUMMARY OF CHAPTER 5

In this chapter, we have presented and discussed the important emerging concept of borders in cultural psychology. First, we have defined bordering as a ubiquitous process that produces a co-genetic system based on the three moments of meaning-making, distinction-making, and value-adding. Borders are forms of organization of the experience and can be material or immaterial, permanent or temporary, more or less permeable. Second, we have discussed the concept of borders as signs that are part of a semiotic activity. Thus, they are subject to interpretation and become part of psychic life through cycles of internalization and externalizations. Then, we have discussed the concept of *Gegenstand* and its implication for development and education. Finally, we have presented the general genetic law of bordering development, showing how borders appear for the first time at the inter-psychological level (in social interactions, as artifacts, as environmental affordances), and appear a second time at the intra-psychological level as regulatory signs. Elaborating the concept of borders, generally understood as a mainly social and physical phenomenon, to a systemic co-genetic and developmental concept is useful to understand a number of psycho-socio-cultural phenomena in everyday life.

Check your knowledge and reflect

Task: How do you experience borders in your everyday life? After reading this chapter, try to reflect on the concept of borders, cogenetic logic, *Gengenstand*, etc. using your personal experience as a starting point. Write a short essay (maximum two pages) elaborating your personal view and using the concepts presented so far. Then, share your essay with two colleagues and ask for their feedback.

NOTES

1 The ideas for this chapter are based on Tateo and Marsico (2021).

2 In analogy with Vygotsky's genetic law of cultural development considering the sociogenesis of bordering psychic function (Vygotsky, 1997).

REFERENCES

Ansaloni, F., &Tedeschi, M. (2016). Understanding space ethically through affect and emotion: From uneasiness to fear and rage in the city. *Emotion, Space and Society*, *21*, 15–22.

Brambilla, C. (2015). Exploring the critical potential of the borderscapes concept. *Geopolitics*, *20*(1), 14–34. http://doi.org/10.1080/14650045.2014.884561

Chaudhary, N., Hviid, P., Marsico, G., & Villadsen, J. (2017). *Resistance in everyday life. Constructing cultural experiences*. Cham: Springer.

Cornell, T. J. (1975). Aeneas and the twins: The development of the roman foundation legend. *Proceedings of the Cambridge Philological Society*, new series *21*(201), pp. 1–32.

Eason, P. K., Cobbs, G. A., & Trinca, K. G. (1999). The use of landmarks to define territorial boundaries. *Animal Behaviour*, *58*(1), 85–91.

Havighurst, R. J. (1948). *Developmental tasks and education*. Chicago, IL: University of Chicago Press.

James, W. (1950). *The principles of psychology*, vol. 1. Mineola, NY: Dover Publications.

Lambert, L. (2015). Remus has to die. *Continent*, *4*(3), 10–11.

Marsico, G. (2011). The "non-cuttable" space in between: Context, boundaries and their natural fluidity. *IPBS: Integrative Psychological and Behavioral Science*, *45*(2), 185–193. https://doi.org/10.1007/s12124-011-9164-9

Marsico, G. (2016). The borderland. *Culture & Psychology*, *22*(2), 206–215. https://doi.org/10.1177/1354067X15601199

Marsico, G., Cabell, K. R., Valsiner, J., & Kharlamov, N. A. (2013). Interobjectivity as a border: The fluid dynamics of "Betweenness". In G. Sammut, P. Daanen, & F. Moghaddam (Eds.), *Understanding the self and others: Explorations in intersubjectivity and interobjectivity* (pp. 51–65). London: Routledge.

Marsico, G., & Tateo, L. (2017). Borders, tensegrity and development in dialogue. *Integrative Psychological and Behavioral Science*, *51*, 536–556.

Marsico, G., & Varzi, A. (2016). Psychological and social borders: Regulating relationships. In J. Valsiner, G. Marsico, N. Chaudhary, T. Sato, & V. Dazzani (Eds.), *Psychology as a science of human being: The Yokohama Manifesto, Annals of Theoretical Psychology*, *13*, (pp. 327–335), Geneva: Springer.

Meinong, A. (1983). *On assumptions*. Berkeley, CA: University of California Press.

Philippopoulos-Mihalopoulos, A. (2013). Atmospheres of law: Senses, affects, lawscapes. *Emotion, Space and Society*, *7*, 35–44.

Picione, R. D. L. (2021). Models of semiotic borders in psychology and their implications: From rigidity of separation to topological dynamics of connectivity. *Theory & Psychology*, *31*(5), 729–745.

Picione, R. D. L., Marsico, G., Tateo, L., & Valsiner, J. (2022). Generalized semiotic functions of borders' model: Contributions from cultural psychology, semiotics and psychoanalysis towards the understanding of borders in human experience. *International Journal of Psychoanalysis and Education: Subject, Action & Society*, *2*(2), 81–111.

Scott, A. L. (1993). A beginning theory of personal space boundaries. *Perspectives in Psychiatric Care*, *29*(2), 12–21.

Simmel, G. (1918/2010). *The view of life: Four metaphysical essays with journal aphorisms*. Trans. J. Andrews. Chicago, IL: University of Chicago Press.

Simmel, G. (1994). Bridge and door. *Theory, Culture & Society*, 11(5), 5–10.

Tateo, L (2016). Toward a cogenetic cultural psychology. *Culture & Psychology*, 22(3), 433–447.

Tateo, L., & Marsico, G. (2019). Framing a theory of ordinary and extraordinary in cultural psychology. In G. Marsico, & L. Tateo (Eds.), *Ordinary things and their extraordinary meanings* (pp. xi–xxix). Charlotte, NC: Information Age.

Tateo, L., & Marsico, G. (2021). Signs as borders and borders as signs. *Theory & Psychology*, 31(5), 708–728.

Tateo, L., & Marsico, G. (2022). Sensing the city: Affective semiosis and urban border-zones. In S. Petrilli & M. Ji (Eds.), *Intersemiotic perspectives on emotions* (pp. 196–209). New York: Routledge.

Valsiner, J. (2001). *Comparative study of human cultural development*. Madrid: Fund. Infancia y Aprendizaje.

Valsiner, J. (2014). Functional reality of the quasi-real: Gegenstandstheorie and cultural psychology today. *Culture & Psychology*, 20(3), 285–307.

Vygotsky, L. S. (1987). Thinking and speech, in *L. S. Vygotsky, Collected works, Volume 1* (pp. 39–285). New York: Plenum. (Edited by R. Rieber and A. Carton; translated by N. Minick.)

Vygotsky, L. S. (1997). The history of the development of higher mental functions. In R. W. Rieber (Ed.), *The collected works of L. S. Vygotsky Vol. 4: The history of the development of higher mental functions*. New York: Plenum Press.

Vygotsky, L. S. (1998). The problem of age. In R. W. Rieber (Ed.), *The collected works of L. S. Vygotsky Vol. 5: Child Psychology*, 187–206. New York: Plenum Press.

Zavershneva, E., & van der Veer, R. (Eds.). (2018). *Vygotsky's notebooks: A selection* (Vol. 2). Cham: Springer.

CHAPTER 6

The psyche as dynamic totality

Scan the QR-code to access additional materials and watch outstanding international scholars discussing key concepts.

> **LEARNING GOALS**
>
> 1. To learn about the human psyche as a dynamic totality
> 2. To learn how cultural psychology describes psychological experience
> 3. To learn the non-binary and dilemmatic features of dynamic processes
> 4. The learn the concepts of dilemma, tensegrity, ambivalence, and affective logic

CHAPTER OVERVIEW

In this chapter, we will present the idea of the human psyche as a dynamic totality based on affective logic and organized on the principle of tensional stability or tensegrity. We will describe the human experience in terms of non-linear processes that imply ambivalence, tension, and dilemmatic choices. This perspective contrasts with the classical idea of psychological processes as closure-seeking and dissonance-avoiding. The dynamic tension between continuity and discontinuity is fundamental to provide psychological functioning and development.

GROUP ACTIVITY FOR INSTRUCTOR: AFFECTIVATING

The instructor asks the students to go out of the classroom into the open air, to look for small stones, pick two each, and bring them back to the classroom. The students must give a name to each of the two stones and put them on the desk while the lecture continues. After the first break of the lesson, when students come back, the instructor asks them to pick one of the stones and throw the other in the trash bin. Then, the instructor starts a round of discussion asking the students, "why did you pick those stones?", "how did you choose which one to keep?", "how did you feel throwing the other?".

Reflection questions
The purpose of the activity is to experience how the person establishes very quickly an affective relationship with everyday objects, projecting meaning onto them. The instructor can use reflection questions:

- Did the stones have particular qualities?
- Can you recall your thoughts while picking them and throwing them away?
- What was your rationale in choosing the names?
- What happens when one gives names?

Socratic (or Platonic) dialogues are a literary philosophic genre, mostly written by the Greek philosopher Plato (approximately 35), in which Socrates is the main character. The plot usually presents Socrates who tries to show the way to real wisdom by means of the "maieutic method", that is examining taken-for-granted beliefs and concepts by systematically questioning them, to expose and overcome the misconceptions and attain true knowledge.

What type of human being is conceived by cultural psychology? In the previous chapters, we presented the epistemological framework (the meta-code, see Chapter 1), and the methodological cycle (see Chapter 2) used to build knowledge in cultural psychology. Then, we discussed some of the main theoretical concepts such as culture (Chapter 3), imaginative processes (Chapter 4) and bordering (Chapter 5). It is now time to describe how cultural psychology understands the way people make meaning of their own experience based on affective logic, and what are the main concepts used to describe the personal existential experiences. This will illuminate the general conception of human psyche that cultural psychology developed in the last 20 years in dialectical and critical relationship with hegemonic trends in psychology.

ARE HUMAN BEINGS COHERENT?

We can start by asking: what type of human being is conceived by hegemonic general psychology (meta-code)? As there are many meta-codes in psychology, we shall look back at ancient Greek philosophy – to Plato's Socratic dialogue "Phaedrus" (Nichols, 1998) in particular. In the dialogue, Plato described his conception of the nature of the human soul through the metaphor of a chariot pulled by two winged horses. The chariot represented the person in their lifelong journey. The charioteer represented intellect, morality, and reason. One horse represented rational or moral impulses or the positive part of a passionate nature (e.g., disinterested friendship, righteous indignation, etc.); while the other represented the irrational passions, appetites, concupiscence. The task of the charioteer was to drive both horses in the same direction and to proceed towards enlightenment. The metaphor established a dualistic representation of human soul/psyche in a continuous struggle between rationality and emotionality, between morality and drives. Of course, it also established a hierarchy among the psychic functions, with intellect and reason as the leading parts (the charioteer). Since then, the normative psychological model has valued rationality over other dimensions (Smelser, 1998). The rationality combined with the idea of agency (Swindell, 2010) established a hierarchy between two opposite fields. On the one hand, there is the idea that humans strive for consistency, balance, clarity, reduction of uncertainty and dissonance, and morality that can be attained through rationality and reflectivity (Yahya & Sukmayadi, 2020). The opposite field is populated by emotions, irrationality, vagueness, dissonance, ambivalence, etc. To allow psychology to be a science of prediction and control of human behavior it was thus necessary to elaborate the idea of a human being whose behavior was somehow consequentially based on given premises. This led to the elaboration of an abstract model of the epistemic agent who naturally tended toward perfect rationality and the self-interest choice, considering the information available (Sturgeon, 2020). The optimal capability of logical reasoning is disgracefully limited by the person's prior beliefs, emotions, self-image, social influence, and habits that cause fallacies (Evans, 2020; Gigerenzer, 2020). The alternative model is the psychoanalytic individual for whom the "horse" of the impulse and passion is constantly trying to make the chariot deviate from its virtuous path. The charioteer's control creates a constant tension that can be resolved only through its verbal transformation, elaboration, and translation into the realm of consciousness and rationality (Freud, 1926; Hill, 2015). Nevertheless, also in this case, the outcome of the process must be a sort of resolution: ambivalence, uncertainty, openness produce anxiety and cannot be tolerated. No matter which horse is stronger and how difficult the charioteer's task is, psychic events in traditional psychology can be represented as a minimal converging branching unit of alternative choices (Figure 6.1).

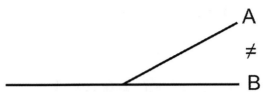

Figure 6.1 Minimal psychic event according to mainstream psychology

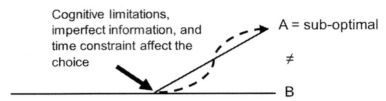

Figure 6.2 Minimal psychic event according to bounded rationality

Psychology follows Aristotelian logic. Thus, alternative "A" is necessarily different from "B" – that, is the alternatives are mutually exclusive. Standing on the bifurcation point between "A" and "B" can only be a temporary condition as its indeterminacy and dissonance cause anxiety. If humans were ideal beings, they would always choose according to perfect rationality and self-interest. Unfortunately, humans are "flawed", and their cognitive capabilities are limited. So, their choice between "A" and "B" will always be sub-optimal (Gigerenzer, 2020). This is the kernel of most cognitive theories, as for instance *bounded rationality theory* (Figure 6.2) (Evans, 2020; Gigerenzer, 2020).

The ideal model of a sub-rational agent is required to fit into a theory of behavior prediction and control. In other words, without establishing a priori baseline normative conditions it would be impossible to calculate the deviance from the expected behavior. Is that what human beings really experience in their existence?

DILEMMAS

In everyday life, rather than a linear process of decision formation, we experience dilemmatic situations – a condition that cannot be described in terms of a branching decision tree. A dilemma is a field of different overlapping potential courses of action (or non-action) that immediately evoke their counterpart according to co-genetic logic (see Chapter 1). Instead of considering all the non-logical aspects as interferences, limitations, or biases, cultural psychology acknowledges that the multidimensional dilemmatic field always includes an affective dimension (feeling glad, disappointed, satisfied, regretting, etc.); an ethical dimension (was worth it, was a waste of time, was an honest price, etc.); and a cognitive dimension (how the phrasing of the problem framed the elaboration of the choice, the meta-cognitive process of re-evaluating afterwards, etc.).

Another difference between a tree-like and a dilemma-like situation, is that while in the former the correct course of action can be established a priori and assessed a posteriori with respect to some gains and losses, in the latter there is no correct choice in absolute terms as the alternative courses of action maintain some degree of presence even after a considerable time. Seldom do the ideas present themselves in our mind as clear and distinct and we always need the contribution of others in order to get a grip on reality through dialogue (Silva Filho et al., 2023). Clarity, definition of mutual excluding alternatives, binary logic, causality, directionality, and closure are all features of a tree-like process that is not attainable in the human everyday experience.

> It is communicated in various dichotomies, freedom versus constraint, independence versus dependence, autonomy versus dependence, maturity versus infancy, and more but whatever the dichotomy, the dilemma appears to be insoluble. Neither pole is a separate state or condition. Neither freedom nor dependence can be realized in a full or exclusive form, because one is part of the other. Human beings long and strive for both, but, when they achieve a measure of either, the other reasserts itself. As in the nature of ambivalence itself, we want both sides at once, but cannot fully satisfy either side.
>
> (Smelser, 1998, p. 15)

A dilemmatic situation is indeed characterized by fuzziness, contemporary presence of cognitive, affective, ethical dimensions, mutually defining (not mutually exclusive) alternative courses of action, persistence over time. The meaning of the dilemma does not disappear once a choice is made. A dilemma implies the production and overcoming of a *Gegenstand* (see Chapter 5).

Just try to imagine the following scenario: you have just graduated from high school and now it is time to choose your higher education. Your parents would like you to become a lawyer or a doctor, but your school counsellor has suggested you take up engineering because you are good at math. You instead dream of becoming a schoolteacher. This can be a very common situation in people's lives. You have a lot of discussions with your parents, you seek your friends' advice. You search for more information about the different career opportunities and the best universities. This is a typical dilemmatic situation because there is no *a priori* optimal choice. The alternatives are not mutually exclusive, they rather *imply* each other co-genetically (Figure 6.3).

In this mental experiment, you can easily realize how it is not only a cognitive task, but also involves affective and ethical issues, fears, desires,

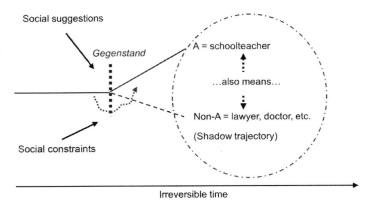

Figure 6.3 Dilemmatic field

Lawrence Kohlberg (1927–1987) was an American psychologist who developed a theory of stages of moral development corresponding to a sociogenetic sequence of progressively more inclusive social circles (family, peers, community, etc.) within which humans seek to be competent members. For Kohlberg, moral development goes from childish and selfish obedience for fear of punishment to mature understanding of the universal principles of human ethics.

expectations, pressures, and requirements (social suggestions and constraints in Figure 6.3). The fact itself of inclining toward alternative "A" ("becoming X") calls into existence the other choices "non-A" ("becoming X" implies "not becoming a Y, Z, etc."). The *Gegenstand* produces a dance of direction and resistance (see Figure 5.4 in Chapter 5) that leads to several possible circumvention strategies (dotted arrow in Figure 6.3). The elements of the dilemmatic field call on each other ("I can do (or be) X but won't do (or be) Y"; "I cannot do (or be) X but will do (or be) Y"; "I cannot do and won't do Y"; "I can do X and will do X"; "I cannot do X now but . . ."; "I could do X now but . . ."; "I could do like (someone else) but . . ."; "I cannot do like (someone else) but . . .", etc.).

Let's continue the mental experiment. The academic year is approaching, you make up your mind and take the education program. However, the dilemma is not dissolved once the choice is made, and the non-actualized ("non-A") alternatives persist as "shadow trajectories" (de Sousa Bastos, 2017). Later in your life, you can experience, with different intensity, the *presence* of the *absent* choice, not necessarily as regret but as co-definition of meaning: you will be the schoolteacher who did not become a lawyer (dotted circle in Figure 6.3) and this will flavor your life choices with a unique quality. In the field-like dilemmatic situations, the choice's meaning is not merely defined by gains and losses but by the whole of the relationships between the elements of the field.

An important use of dilemmas in psychology was established by Lawrence Kohlberg (1981) to study moral development. Kohlberg was indeed interested in how people made sense of their moral choices and the values they appealed to justify their moral decisions. He created the following dilemmatic scenario:

> A woman was on her deathbed. There was one drug that the doctors said would save her. It was a form of radium that a druggist in the same

town had recently discovered. The drug was expensive to make, but the druggist was charging ten times what the drug cost him to produce. He paid $200 for the radium and charged $2,000 for a small dose of the drug. The sick woman's husband, Heinz, went to everyone he knew to borrow the money, but he could only get together about $1,000 which is half of what it cost. He told the druggist that his wife was dying and asked him to sell it cheaper or let him pay later. But the druggist said: 'No, I discovered the drug and I'm going to make money from it.' So, Heinz got desperate and broke into the man's laboratory to steal the drug for his wife. Should Heinz have broken into the laboratory to steal the drug for his wife? Why or why not?

Depending on the stage of moral development, the person would justify the choice of stealing or not with different reasons. The person in a more mature developmental stage would appeal to more abstract and general moral principles while the person at an earlier stage would use more opportunistic reasons. Kohlberg believed in the universality and sequentiality of the developmental stages, although not in their rigid temporal frame, including the fact that a person could regress to an earlier stage under some conditions. Kohlberg's theory was clearly "platonic": his charioteer is inherently eudemonic, capable of reason, and striving to understand the others and the world around them. Nevertheless, when Shweder and Much (1987) tried to use Heinz's dilemma in a different cultural context, namely India, they found that Kohlberg's assumptions were not universal. For their Indian respondents, there was no dilemma actually. Indeed, stealing the drug was not an option that the respondent took into consideration (Shweder & Much, 1987). This example shows the *Gegenstand* nature of dilemmatic choices (see Chapter 5): something becomes a border (e.g., a difficult moral choice to adopt an illegal conduct) only when the person's intentionality is directed toward it (see Figure 5.3 in Chapter 5). Shweder and Much's (1987) respondent did not have difficulty imagining an alternative solution to the inadmissibility of stealing: "He may not get the medicine by stealing. He may sell himself. He may sell himself to someone for say 500 rupees for 6 months or 1 year" (Shweder & Much, 1987, p. 236). Hence, the emphasis is on the personal agency and the moral imperative of the responsibility to find a solution *without harming others*: "the idea of the Self in a moral sense is deeply personal and individual" (Chaudhary et al., 2022, p. 11). The dilemmatic field is neither universal nor context-independent, but it is an arena in which personal and collective cultural meanings interact in the form of vectorial forces (see Figure 5.3) producing a dynamic tension.

When I produce a discourse about my feeling guilty or anguished, I can say that I feel 'like' Rodion Raskolnikov in Dostoyevsky's novel *Crime and Punishment*. I can also say that I feel 'like' my friend felt once. But at the same time, I am conscious that my feeling is a unique event that is not perfectly framed in a pre-formed fashion or captured by the same signs already used by myself or by others in the past. 'Humans consist of present, future, and past; sign, interpretant, and act; I, you, and me; and all the overlap, and connectedness, and solidarity among these elements.'

(Tateo & Marsico, 2013, p. 5)

What was missing in Kohlberg's model is the consideration of the persistence of the dilemmatic field before and beyond the specific event of the decision making. The dilemma is interpreted by the person through "projective contextualizations – the insertion of previously established meanings into the current context" (Abbey, 2004, p. 333), what in semiotic terms could be called the habits of the interpretant. For instance, in the university dilemma mental experiment, the person may think "I imagine myself like a *good* schoolteacher, but my parents or friends could think that I am a *loser* because I did not have *higher expectations*". According to Abbey (2004), "the individual, projecting internalized general social knowledge" (p. 333) produces the meanings "good", "loser", "higher expectations" that were not necessarily related to the original problem. This creates a tension between opposite and conflicting meanings that is experienced as a form of *ambivalence*.

Paul Eugen Bleuler (1857–1939) was a Swiss psychiatrist who coined several psychiatric terms including "schizophrenia", "schizoid", "autism", "depth psychology", and "ambivalence".

AMBIVALENCE

The term ambivalence in psychiatry was introduced by Eugen Bleuler in his study on schizophrenia (Bleuler, 1911/1950). Among the four main symptoms of schizophrenia, *ambivalence* is the "tendency to endow the most diverse psychisms with both a positive and negative indicator at the same time" (Bleuler, 1911/1950, 53). According to Bleuler, people relate to the objects that have inherently dual aspects, like the rose and the thorn: "pleasant and unpleasant feelings simultaneously accompany the same experience" (Graubert & Miller, 1957, p. 458). Usually, people can construct a set of associations in thoughts to evaluate the good and the bad, and respond quickly to an object in the most appropriate way. Due to a reduced capacity of forming emotionally loaded associations, schizophrenic people are unable to resolve the relationship with the object. Attaching opposite emotions to an object is a feature of all people, who under normal conditions are nevertheless able to cope with those emotions when required (Abbey, 2004; Bleuler, 1911/1950). Bleuler (1911/1950) distinguished three dimensions of ambivalence:

- *affective ambivalence*: opposing feeling can be related to the same object, like hating and loving the partner at the same time.
- *ambivalence of the will*: implies both the desires of doing and not doing a certain thing at the same time.

- *intellectual ambivalence*: a disorder of thought in which one idea is accompanied by its opposite.

In Bleuler's theory, ambivalence was a condition of experience in both normal and pathological relationships to objects. Thus, people are usually coping with ambivalence in the construction of the self but this can happen "at different levels of consciousness" (Graubert & Miller, 1957, p. 458). Bleuler's multidimensional idea of ambivalence (cognitive, affective, and agentic) was later reduced to specific dimensions of ambivalence.

For instance, Sigmund Freud (1955) developed the theory of ambivalence that will become a point of reference. Freud's theory of drives considered ambivalence at the level of affects and ideas that share the same energy and are developed in pairs, with one polarity displaced into the unconscious without being completely resolved. This distribution is crystallized and subject to the culturally guided collective mechanism of elaboration. Nevertheless, it is always possible that in the development of the drive its antagonist reappears from the repressed and persists, leading to ambivalence. At the level of the drive content, the same object (e.g., a parent, a love partner, but also a car, a career achievement, etc.) can be invested with opposite coexisting drives such as love and hate (Graubert & Miller, 1957). Freud's idea of ambivalence is restricted to the specific field of the drives' system, where opposite tendencies always coexist. The psychic labor consists of finding a balance between the two manifestations of psychic energy through a choice that must come to pact with the cultural constraints, that is the social suggestions about how it is acceptable to feel towards something. Hence, human beings struggle with a constellation of opposing drives, negotiating with the internalized culture over which one among them is acceptable. The nonacceptable drives are repressed but not eliminated, ready to come back in the form of creative (through sublimation) or disruptive (as neurosis or psychosis) outcomes.

Other people as objects of affection are also inherently ambivalent because they are *Gegenstanden*. They do not simply sit there being subject to our directional impulse, but they establish dialogical relationships with us. *Gegenstanded* are indeed responsive (see Chapter 2) and as much as we strive for them, they exert a grip on us in return.

The role of significant Others in the concept of ambivalence has been elaborated in attachment theory (Ainsworth et al., 1978). According to this theory, ambivalence is part of a homeostatic model in which the opposite infant drives of exploration and security are experienced by child–mother pairs in search of balance as the desirable outcome. If the mother is not supporting the resolution of ambivalence, the infant can develop a problematic anxious–ambivalent attachment style. Attachment theory shows how the mother is the first social partner through which the infant can learn that other people are only partially predictable. Conversely, children can also suffer when people are *totally* predictable. A certain degree of ambivalence is thus functional to development. "Childrearing tends to be imperfect because with each of its particular acts it must serve two opposed tendencies: freeing and binding" (Simmel, 1918/2010, p. 177).

The homeostatic view of psyche understood ambivalence as a perturbation of equilibrium, at the level of drives, as in the case of Freud and Ainsworth, at the level of logical inconsistencies, or at the level of communication and intersubjectivity.

Cognitive ambivalence has been studied in cognitive philosophy and psychology. According to Swindell (2010), ambivalence can appear at two levels: difficulty in forming a position in identifying the individual will (e.g., establishing a hierarchy or priority between diverging desires), or the moral stance toward a desire (e.g., deciding whether a desire is legitimate or not). Ambivalence can also occur at the level of forming a will and taking a decision to act despite having identified the correct order of the desires. Going back to our previous example of the university's choice, one can experience ambivalence when establishing the hierarchy of alternatives (e.g., "what do I really want to prioritize, my desire to be a teacher or my economic success"). Once one priority is identified, ambivalence can be experienced at a moral level ("I feel it is right to prioritize my desire but also feel guilty"). Finally, one can experience ambivalence at the moment of taking action based on a desire ("the day I go to sign up, I will hesitate when signing the papers"). At each level, different desires are invested with affective charge and ambivalence can present itself at different magnitudes: it can go from a small hesitation to enacting the decision, to the paralyzing ambivalence of being completely unable to form a hierarchy of preferences.

In cognitive psychology, ambivalence is defined in terms of:

a) *objective ambivalence*: that "represents the actual presence of conflicting evaluative reactions within a given person (i.e., having both positive and negative reactions towards the same object)"
b) *subjective ambivalence*: "the experience of evaluative conflict, including a sense of being conflicted, confused, torn, and mixed with regard to the attitude object."

(DeMarree et al., 2014, p. 6)

Studying the construct of "attitudes", research showed that two-dimensional models of attitude scales where unable to grasp the phenomenon because attitudes toward an object could not simply be measured in terms of positive–negative polarities. Kaplan (1972) proposed splitting the attitude scales into two different subscales, each measuring the positive and negative polarities of the object. The problem was not limited to bi-polar reactions to an object but to different levels of organization, because ambivalence implied a cognitive level with mixed reactions; an affective level of conflicting feelings; and a behavioral level of decision making (DeMarree et al., 2014). The affective and behavioral level were reduced to the cognitive level: the disquieting and contrasting feeling and the difficulty in acting depended on the need for a correct and consistent appraisal of the situation. People experience ambivalence when they cannot produce a consistent account of the object and their relationship to it. When they cannot reduce the dissonance or incongruence between the perceived and expected situation (Albarracin, Zanna & Blair, 2005).

The anthropologist Gregory Bateson captured the inherent ambivalence of human relationships with the *double bind theory* (Bateson, 1972; Bateson et al., 1956). The double bind is a specific interpersonal situation in which the individual is unable to resolve a communication dilemma based on the conflict between different logic levels (Bateson et al., 1956). The double bind concept is related to the impossibility of escaping from an ambivalent situation, which can lead to mental distress and be part of the schizophrenia's aetiology (Bateson, 1972). The double bind is ambivalent at the levels of the message (opposite injunctions of different order and polarity); the power relationship (one participant must have some power of constriction over the other as well as an affective relation); the level of logic inconsistency (the injunctions lead to incompatible outcomes); the affective level (feelings of attraction and repulsion); and the level of meaning (impossibility to make sense of the situation and elaborate a solution). The typical double bind situation can occur in family or romantic relationships, but it can also be frequent in educational settings (Tateo, 2018a). Examples of double bind messages are a caregiver who says, "You know I love you" while punishing or physically repulsing the subject; a teacher who says "You must be motivated!" or "You must be creative!" to the students while those are complex processes that you cannot simply commanded yourself to do. The double bind situation can also be functional to the system homeostasis or the maintenance of the *status quo* (Bateson et al., 1956). In contrast to other ideas on ambivalence, for Bateson it is an attribute of the whole situation rather than an incapability of the individual to resolve inner conflicts between opposite feelings. The only way to make sense of it and to escape the meaning trap is to make explicit the ambiguity of the situation through a metacommunicative act. In terms of cultural psychology (see Chapter 1), to escape the double bind it is necessary to produce a sign at a higher hierarchical level that can defuse the trap by canceling the effect of the previous conflicting signs (e.g., "I cannot be creative just because you ask me to be!").

The different definitions of ambivalence discussed so far challenge the normative model of a rational agent used in psychology. Ambivalence is not due to the subject's limited perceptual, cognitive, and affective characteristics. Harrist (2006) claimed that the rationalist assumptions in psychology reinforced the idea that experiencing ambivalence is bad. Instead, ambivalence is a condition of life in which "multiple feelings lead to experiences of ambivalence moving from background, to disorientation, exploration, resolution

Gregory Bateson (1904–1980) was an English anthropologist, social scientist, linguist, semiotician, and cyberneticist. He developed the double-bind theory of schizophrenia. He also developed important ideas in ecological anthropology.

and back again" (Harrist, 2006, p. 110). Ambivalence is also an attribute of the interpersonal relationships (Bateson, 1972), and of every form of social organization (e.g. family, school, group of peers, political parties) inscribed in a system of value-oriented practices that contain contradictory elements. In school, for instance, one can easily find ambivalent messages like "become independent" and "obey your teacher". These are not pathological forms of miscommunication, as in the double bind case, rather ordinary examples of how ambivalence constitutes experiencing (Tateo, 2018a).

THE SEMIOTICS OF AMBIVALENCE

To understand why ambivalence is important for the psyche we can turn once again to semiotics. Every organism develops and survives only in a relationship of exchange with its environment. The exchange is not only in terms of nurturing, but also in terms of semiosis. Indeed, organisms use elements of their environment "as building blocks in their development towards new skills and cognitive capacities" (Maran, 2020, p. 36). This is also the principle of the sociogenesis of higher mental functions in humans (see Chapter 1). It means that an organism is cannot be separated by its environment, which provides "counters-structures, constraints, or boundary conditions for normal functioning" (Maran, 2020, p. 36). In other words, the environment sets *windows of acceptable possibilities* (see Chapter 3). Those relations with "others are essentially dialogic as they work through expressing, making use of, responding, and accommodating" (Maran, 2020, p. 36). The human environment is cultural (see Chapter 3) and the interactions occur through different types of signs (see Chapter 1) that can be more or less conventional but still require some sort of common ground that makes communication possible. However, a relationship based only on common ground would be useless for the development. In a productive dialogue, "some cracks need to be opened in the symbolic system, some inconsistencies need to emerge through which more spontaneous sign activities can unfold and the other agencies can enter semiosis" (Maran, 2020, p. 37). In other words, without a certain degree of ambivalence, semiosis is impossible because there is no room for signs interpretation: "increasing and decreasing levels of ambivalence construct a self-perpetuating process of meaning construction and emergence of signs with a number of different conditions" (Abbey & Valsiner, 2005, p. 6). "All signs contain an element of certainty – the part of the meaning that 'feels right' at the present – which is quickly taking a form expected from the future" (Abbey & Valsiner, 2005, p. 6). Thus, all signs also contain a part of uncertainty. But we can also say that a sign "A" implies its complementary part "non-A" (see Chapter 1), or that each sign has a non-imaginative part (certainty) and an imaginative part (openness, uncertainty) (see Chapter 4).

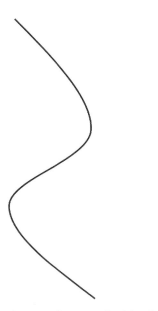

Figure 6.4 The co-genetic triplet obtained by drawing a border (see Chapter 5)

The minimal unit of ambivalence is already the basic co-genetic triplet (Figure 6.4).

By drawing a simple curvilinear segment, we immediately generate a co-genetic triplet (see Chapter 5). This simple sign contains an element of perceptual ambivalence to the extent that the curvilinearity suggests but does not make explicit a differential value in its parts. In such a simple situation, the minimal ambivalence of the triplet can be tolerated or ignored. However, one can easily suggest a specific direction of meaning-making by introducing a simple element of differentiation between the subparts (Figure 6.5).

This very simple semiotic act is at the basis of the human phenomenon of *sensuality* to the extent that it generates *Gestalten* at different levels (Valsiner, 2020; Valsiner & Rudolph, 2017).

Figure 6.6 shows the increasing Gestalt level (Valsiner & Rudolph, 2017) compared to Figure 6.5. Nevertheless, the sensuality of the image and aesthetic pleasure are preserved as far as the complex of signs that form the drawing as a whole still possess a certain degree of ambivalence, requiring an aesthetic cooperative interpretation between the artist, the drawing, and the audience.

Abbey and Valsiner (2005) show how ambivalence is inherent to semiosis but to different degrees. It can be low and can be accepted ("it can be X … it can be Y") or ignored ("but I don't care"). In this case, no new meanings are required. The ambivalence intensifies when individuals realize that what

THE PSYCHE AS DYNAMIC TOTALITY

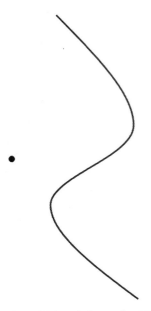

Figure 6.5 Introducing a value differential

Figure 6.6 *Corpulent nude woman* – drawing by Edward Nagle (1920) (MET, 1984.433.258), public domain image (https://commons.wikimedia.org/wiki/File:Corpulent_Nude_Woman_MET_sf1984.433.258.jpg)

they think they know is not sufficient in relation to what they know they do not understand. When ambivalence reaches its higher level, two things may happen. On the one hand, the person can demolish the existing signs and start from scratch ("I don't know anything") or alternatively can produce "momentarily stable signs that mediate uncertainty by pre-controlling the meaning of a situation" (Abbey & Valsiner, 2005, p. 10) ("yes, it must be X!").

Socrates' maieutic method, as reported in the Platonic dialogue that opened this chapter, pointed exactly at escalating ambivalence through systematic questioning until his interlocutor reached a point of bifurcation. In the lines below from Phaedrus, we can see how it unfolded micro-genetically (Nichols, 1998).

i. Socrates: When anyone speaks of iron and silver, is not the same thing present in the minds of all?
ii. Phaedrus: Certainly.
iii. Socrates: But when anyone speaks of justice and goodness we part company and are at odds with one another and with ourselves?
iv. Phaedrus: Precisely.
   [. . .]
v. Socrates: I cannot help fancying in my ignorance that he wrote off boldly just what came into his head, but I dare say that you would recognize a rhetorical necessity in the succession of the several parts of the composition?
vi. Phaedrus: You have too good an opinion of me if you think that I have any such insight into his principles of composition.

There is a difference between Socrates' question in line "i" and in line "iii". While the first implied a zero degree of ambivalence, the question in line "iii" is slightly more debatable. However, Phaedrus' answer in line "iv" is of the type "yes, it must be X!". Later in the dialogue, Socrates' questions escalate in openness and complexity, leaving more space to ambivalence like in line "v". Hence, Phaedrus' answer in line "vi" is of the type "I don't know anything" (Abbey & Valsiner, 2005). As in the case of double bind, the only way to escape Socrates' semiotic trap would be to move upward in the hierarchy of signs and engage in a metacommunicative activity. Indeed, Socrates' questions do not involve a dialogue at the level of definitions, and Phaedrus experienced ambivalence because he did not realize that Socrates was discussing the *method* of dialoguing.

The maieutic method also shows that ambivalence is not an inherent feature of signs alone. Indeed, Socrates used quite simple and mundane words. Ambivalence is rather a property of the person–context systemic organization in which the alternatives and their opposites are called into existence at the same time. The elaboration of meaning in response to the ambivalence is produced only in relationship with the Other. As the ambivalent message contained in the smoking sing in Figure 3.5 of Chapter 3, the context includes the social suggestions and constraints that operate at the bifurcation point (Figure 6.3). Social suggestions and constraints represent a large part of what people think that they know about something (i.e., the common-sense knowledge Socrates evokes in line "i"). This is the window of acceptable possibilities, involving in a single circumstance the conditions for functioning and the acceptable range of uncertainty and ambiguity that the system can tolerate without being affected. The rules and condition for the violation of the rules are both evoked at the same time.

> Certain sorts of deviant behavior are highly valuable, others are not. The former is usually called creative and is supported (in normal times) as long as it remains within bounds; the latter is called destructive. If we assume that the highest educational priority is placed on creativity, then special environments within which to pursue creativity must be constructed (recognized as open systems); otherwise the stabilizing forces of 'normal' schooling will 'normalize' (destroy) emerging creativity.
> (Sawada & Caley, 1985, p. 17)

So far, discussing the concepts of the dilemmatic field and ambivalence, we have presented a different way of understanding meaning-making. The need for consistency, closure, stability, or balance are not the necessary outcome of meaning-making. Openness is not something painful that must be overcome, it is rather the source of novel meanings and the condition for communication.

TENSEGRITY

In the same way psychology does not like ambivalence, it does not like tension. In general terms, psychology has two main abstract models of psychic functioning: the linear cybernetics model (Figure 6.7a); and the dynamic homeostatic model (Figure 6.7b) (Cabell & Valsiner, 2013; DeYoung & Krueger, 2018).

Almost all the theories we find in contemporary psychology can be traced back to these two ways of describing psychic functioning (Cabell & Valsiner, 2013; DeYoung, & Krueger, 2018). In the linear model (Figure 6.7a), an environmental (external) input must somehow be processed and lead to an observable behavior. Psychologists have different understandings of what is happening inside the "black box". The mechanism has been described as network of associations, information elaboration modules, neural networks, systems 1 and 2, etc. In the homeostatic model (Figure 6.7b), the system is in equilibrium when the environmental conditions function within certain parameters that allow a homeostatic exchange between the organism and the

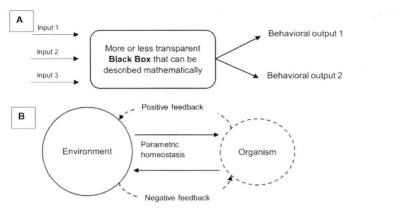

Figure 6.7 Main theoretical models in psychology

environment through feedback mechanisms that buffer minimal variations. This allows the person to not apply all cognitive and emotional resources to solve minimal everyday problems, because minimal variations that fall within identifiable and familiar specimens can be easily adapted.

If a change in the environmental conditions exceeds certain tolerance parameters, the conflict arises between the organism's tendency to maintain a status of equilibrium as long as possible, and to move towards a new equilibrium while the changing conditions of the environment resist such a tendency. According to this model, two outcomes are possible: an adaptation or a rupture that challenges the organism's identity. In this feedback mechanism, one can find the directionality/resistance dynamics described in Chapter 5. The Gestalt theory provides an example of resistance to change and maintaining homeostasis with the Zeigarnik's effect (Zeigarnik, 1967) in which people remember unfinished or interrupted tasks better than completed tasks. Kurt Lewin's field theory (Lewin, 1936; 1939) also conceived human life space – or psychological field – as a space made by several subregions and populated by meaningful objects, each one with its own specific value or charge. These charges generate a field of forces in homeostatic equilibrium (Lewin, 1936; 1939). Every time a person encounters a new object or experience, the psychological field requires adaptation and reconfiguration of the field of forces, unless the change is too relevant to the psychological field differentiates in new subregions.

The main limit of the two models described above is that they account for change only in the presence of an external force acting upon the organism because they are based on a causal model in which change is always exogenous. Besides, they conceptualize the homeostasis as a static condition that requires no energy for its maintenance. In this perspective, all the phenomena of ambivalence, tension, uncertainty represent a form of pressure on the organism that leads to deformation (adaptation or rupture). In the perspective of cultural psychology, however, the human being is an open psychological system that is not only in exchange with the environment as part of a whole, but is also a whole/part system itself. In the field of architecture, Fuller (1961) theorized that a structure organized in terms of whole/parts hierarchical relationship is subject to a field of continuous tension and discontinuous compression, which is called "self-stress" or "prestress". The concept of "tensegrity" (Fuller, 1961), a contraction of "tensional integrity", claims that tension is not a pathology of a system, rather one of its complementary constitutive elements, providing stability and integrity. "As the term 'tensegrity system' implies, the interplay between the tension and compression elements may be interpreted as a whole as systemic behaviour unpredictable from the behaviour of the parts considered individually" (Judge, 1978, p. 261). A typical example of a tensegrity system is a tent, whose integrity is the result of the self-stress between the pulling forces of the ropes and the compression of the poles: without continuous tension, the tent would simply collapse. However, tensegrity is also very common in biological systems such as the human musculoskeletal system.

> Our bodies provide a familiar example of a prestressed tensegrity structure: our bones act like struts to resist the pull of tensile muscles, tendons and ligaments, and the shape stability (stiffness) of our bodies varies depending on the tone (prestress) in our muscles.
> (Ingber, 2003, p. 1158)

The tensegrity principle acts both at the level of the structure and at the level of the sub-parts functions. In a tensegrity system, the sub-parts specialize in functioning as modular sub-systems with their own tensegrity organization, which is functional to the maintenance of the whole.

> It is the unique equilibrium (made possible by a tensegrity pattern) between what unites (i.e., the tensional network) and what divides (i.e. the many distinct compressional incompatibilities) which gives rise to (and derives from) the new kind of organizational structure.
> (Judge, 1978, p. 260)

As we have seen in Chapter 5, the co-genetic triplet ("A"+border+"non-A") is the minimal form of whole/parts organization of the psychic functioning. Thus, environmental pressure does not act on a system in a state of (homeo)static equilibrium, but rather interacts with a self-stressed psychic system that is already in a state of dynamic tensegrity. The tensegrity principle has several implications in the way we understand psychological processes. For instance, tension is never resolved because it is a structural feature of the organism. More specifically, tension is resolved by the fact that the organism maintains its structural organization (Figure 6.8). Tension is to a certain

Environment does not act upon a static equilibrium but interacts with a system that is already in a dynamic tensegrity.

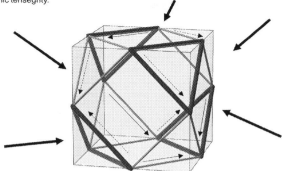

Figure 6.8 Catalytic model

degree part of the labor of maintaining the person's own self-organization, which does not necessarily result in observable behavior (see for instance the importance of grasping non-behavior, or the meaningfulness of silence discussed in Chapter 2). The need for closure and resolution is only one possible outcome in relation to the person's continuous striving for what's next in irreversible time.

Of course, an excessive degree of tension provoked by too much ambivalence is unbearable by the organism and can bring its disruption. The environment provides scaffolding that the organism can use to buffer the tension within certain parameters. Thus, the environment and the social interactions do not directly *cause* something but produce *catalytic conditions* (Cabell & Valsiner, 2013) for a process to ignite and lead to a new whole/part tensegrity condition not completely predictable by the initial conditions of the system. "Catalytic conditions – rather than causal events in life course – guide the formation of one's structured self" (Valsiner, 2021, p. 22). Ambivalence is always a "tension produced by a system entailing a kernel and at least two vectors that are non-isomorphic in size and direction" (Abbey & Valsiner, 2004, 4). One could say that the person is "in tension" because of "intention", that is goal-oriented directionality towards a particular object of experience (see Chapter 5) that also becomes meaningful by virtue of the social constraints attached to it. The environment provides semiotic operators that act as mediators and can temporarily play the role of catalysts of psychic change (Cabell & Valsiner, 2013). Unlike the model in Figure 6.7a, the mediator does not represent a linear cause – it represents an element that changes the system parameters to allow change. Once the process has led to a transformation, the catalyst stops playing an active role but becomes available in the environment. One example of catalytic function is presented by Tania Zittoun (2006) with the concept of symbolic resource. Imagine a person who is experiencing a major change in their life course, for instance the sudden loss of a beloved other. This unexpected event requires the elaboration of new meanings, of new life perspective, of grieving, etc. The person is already in a condition of pre-stress and listens to a particular song that evokes memories, similar stories, whose music provides a specific aesthetic experience. That song becomes a semiotic mediator (symbolic resource) that does not cause any change but creates the conditions for new meaning-making. After the process has led to the new dynamic tensegrity, the role of the semiotic mediator is finished and the symbolic resource can become again a peripheral part of the surrounding environment, ready to be reactivated as operator next time new events require meaning-making. It is a very common experience to encounter these semiotic mediators with catalytic functions both in major life transitions and in smaller everyday events in which we are required to make sense of something. It is important to note also that the signs operating as catalytic mediators are somehow ambivalent. Indeed, the song in the previous event will be invested with a mixed feeling in the future, for instance a sort of bitter–sweet taste of nostalgia.

The idea of the person as a tensegrity psychic system is important because it explains that tension and ambivalence are necessary (within some parameters) for the maintenance of the system itself, as well as to its development. This process is not to be understood as a temporary imbalance that must be overcome or recovered (as the homeostatic model in Figure 6.7b), but as a continuous dynamic and dialogical movement between and within subparts of the person–system and the person–environment system. Because the ambivalent meanings are in tension and at the same time interlinked by co-genetic complementarity, the development of new and flexible configurations is possible. The cultural context will frame this process by promoting some acceptable compromises while inhibiting others.

Most significant life experiences are characterized by those complex affective tonalities. Seldom do we experience simple and isolated emotions. The important things in life are usually experienced with a mix of feelings, sometimes opposites, often ambivalent. Many cultures have special words for those oceanic feelings in which different polarities converge into a whole at a higher level (Figure 6.9).

For the ancient Greeks this experience was represented by the concept of "nostos" (Tateo, 2019); in German the concept of "*Heimat*" has a similar connotation; in Lusophony cultures, the higher-level synthesis is expressed by the complex emotion of "saudade", etc. There are a number of mundane activities that are based on this type of feeling, like watching horror movies (amused to be scared), practicing extreme sports (excited to risk life), betting (happy about risk), eating food with very hot chili peppers (pleasure from painful taste), etc. Tension, ambivalence, and uncertainty are part of existence and most of us are perfectly living with them (within certain parameters). All those feelings share the quality of being more than the sum of their parts (i.e., positive + negative feelings) and cannot thus be simply

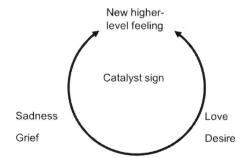

Opposite and ambivalent feelings converge into a new higher-level form through catalyst sign

Figure 6.9 Ambivalent feelings organized in a higher-level meaning

operationalized in psychometrics (remember the problem of measuring attitudes discussed earlier). They are also field-like signs that cannot be completely described through a finite number of properties, and certainly not completely verbalized (Valsiner, 2020; 2021). The human being is the "bordering creature that has no border" (Simmel, 1994, p. 10).

This leads us to the last important feature of the human psyche as cultural psychology views it: meaning originates from the affective relation to the world.

AFFECTIVE LOGIC

The focus on affect and "the study of emotions, moods, preferences, attitudes, value, and stress" (Gross, 1998, p. 997) has been part of "the 'turn to affect' across the humanities and social sciences" (Blackman & Venn, 2010, p. 8) especially about neurological and psychodynamic processes (Blackman & Venn, 2010; Gross, 1998; Williams, 2001). In cultural psychology, the notion of affect is very important.

> It consists of bodily capacities to affect and to be affected that emerge and develop in concert. For example, exhaustion both follows from a worker's position in a process of production and limits what a body can do. This initial definition has one important consequence. Straight away a body is always imbricated in a set of relations that extend beyond it and constitute it. Capacities are always collectively formed [. . .] Second, affect pertains to capacities rather than existing properties of the body. Affects are about what a body may be able to do in any given situation, in addition to what it currently is doing and has done. Because capacities are dependent on other bodies, they can never be exhaustively specified in advance.
>
> (Anderson, 2014, pp. 9–10)

We relate to the world first by prolapsing our feelings into it — both being affected and affecting — and then by projecting a system of hierarchization, semiotization, and organization onto the phenomena through the bordering process (see Chapter 5).

> Affectivating is universal. Every person in the World relates to it in his or her unique personal way — but in all of these ways one feature is common to all — feeling into the particular setting one is in. Our efforts to be 'rational' are the result of our feeling into the World, but not at the starting point. This is a radical break from the rational self image of psychology as science.
>
> (Valsiner, 2021, p. ix)

As we discussed at the beginning of the chapter, for cultural psychology the role of the personal synthesis in psychic life is not an exclusive function of rationality. On the contrary, we apprehend the world as "physiognomies", that is a whole complex of forms expressive of a character, which "provides us with reasons for making certain kinds of responses" (Lennon, 2010, p. 377). The physiognomies (or *Gestalten*) are not defined just by inherent features of the world. They emerge from the dialogical relationship between the person *feeling into* and the environment *responding to* framed by the cultural and social suggestions. In other words, culture is *in between* the person and environment in the form of mediators (inhibitors, catalyzers, promoters) regulating the quality and magnitude of the range of possible semiotic interpretations (ambivalence) within parameters that are not too restrictive or too open.

> The shapes or forms which order our perceptions do not only categorise, but carry emotional significance for us. And this is true of linguistic categories as well as other images and symbols. [. . .] When we perceive other parts of the world as having an affective shape we also perceive them as reason constituting in a parallel way. The world is experienced as a world of possibilities for us, both for intentional projects and expressive responses; those which would be appropriate or make sense, given how the world appears.
>
> (Lennon, 2010, pp. 384–385)

The culture operates in the affectivating process through social suggestions and constraints in the form of signs peripherally present and distributed in the environment as symbolic resources, such as architecture, iconography, rituals, practices, dress-codes, etc. Their purpose is to promote some affects and forms of conduct that the person is expected to experience in each situation, and to inhibit other forms of conduct that are considered inappropriate (Tateo, 2018b) in a window of acceptable possibilities. Nevertheless, experiencing is a personal unique trajectory of meaning-making mediated by signs, although it unfolds in a negotiation with the social suggestions.

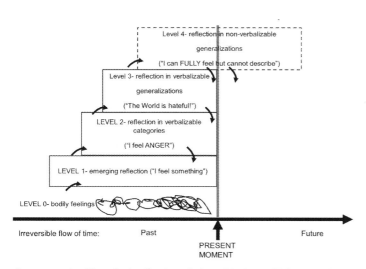

Figure 6.10 Sign hierarchy in affective relating with the world (adapted from Valsiner, 2021, p. 40)

Valsiner (2021) described how signs are produced and interpreted starting from the affective relationship with the world and how they are organized: a "hierarchy starts from the lower-level physiological bodily feeling (Level 0) that is directly triggered by some ongoing life experience" (Valsiner, 2021, p. 38). Figure 6.10 presents the hierarchy of signs progression of the affective semiosis.

The embodied affective encounter triggers the production of what Valsiner (2021) called proto-signs (Level 1) where the bodily feeling gains an approximate meaning (I feel that "I feel something" but cannot name it). As we have seen in the case of ambivalence (Abbey & Valsiner, 2004), if the experience is not particularly relevant or emotional, the process can stop here ("I don't know and don't really care"). Otherwise, the semiosis can develop into signs that identify emotion categories ("I feel happy/sad/angry/etc.") and expressible through categories in ordinary language. Cultural suggestions act at this level, because once a particularly available label has been used, it implies a set of expectations and acceptable non-acceptable directions of feeling ("I feel happy, therefore X"). This further elaboration triggers the co-genetic and dialogical aspects of the meaning and can lead to a generalization through verbal argumentation – in auto and hetero dialogue (see Chapter 3). The label of the emotion escalates into the formation of increasingly abstract and vague but powerful "philosophical" meanings (Level 3).

> Finally, at Level 4 as the field-like signs of Level 3 become hyper-generalized, the verbal accessibility to the meanings vanishes and the person here-and-now feels understanding of the experience in deep intuitive ways which transcend the boundary of the present toward the future. [. . .] Through hyper-generalization, the meanings that emerge in strictly

contextualized circumstances expand in space and time – even beyond the border to the future – and become our meaningful ways of anticipating and flavoring the emerging new present coming out of the future.

(Valsiner, 2021, p. 40)

The process of affective generalization can occur either in a de-escalating top-down or in an escalating bottom-up direction. The top-down direction consists of framing the personal experience through a hyper-generalized sign and selectively internalizing some social suggestions about how it "ought" to be experienced. The person is expressing some selective forms of conduct in return (e.g., dressing in black during mourning; avoiding some foods during a period; etc.) that orient the personal affective experience. The public display of intra-psychological state feeds into the externalization of signs to the immediate environment. For instance, in many societies, the concept of marital fidelity is represented by a specific artifact: usually a ring. The act of wearing the ring for the first time (irreversible time) produces an embodied affective experience (level 0). The ring is the representamen of a clear hyper-generalized sign "marital fidelity". The public display of the ring produces a message to the environment ("I am faithful"). The cultural concept of fidelity feeds in return into the intra-psychological world, creating a socially guided affective experience ("I feel faithful") (Figure 6.11).

In terms of affective logic, the two statements "I am faithful to my spouse *therefore* I wear the wedding ring" and "I wear the wedding ring *therefore* I am faithful to my spouse" are equally valid. Besides, "marital fidelity" is meaningful as it is related to "non-fidelity" as an unrealized but meaningful sub-part of the referent ("I am faithful"; "I am non-non-faithful"). The hyper-generalized sign "marital fidelity" thus works as a window of acceptable possibilities (what can be, what ought to be, what is not allowed to be, etc.). It is related to different systems of values such as medical discourse (prolificacy, life expectancy, etc.) or religious discourse (sin, holiness of marriage, etc.)

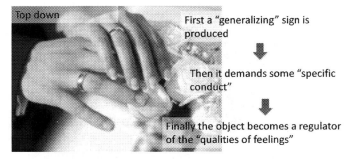

Figure 6.11 The artifact as a hyper-generalized sign orients affective experience (Tateo, 2018b)

that promote or inhibit a range of potential future trajectories (the arrows towards the future at level 4 in Figure 6.10). Postmodern societies display increasing multiplication and diversity of social suggestions opening new windows of acceptable possibilities, but also weakening the specific social suggestions of a certain community. In terms of affective logic, "marital fidelity" is also defined *through* the complementary meaning of "non-marital fidelity" and feeds into the emerging meaning of "non-non-fidelity". This complex of meanings opens the possibility of the production of new meanings that can result in various forms of "marital non-infidelity" as we eventually observe in people's everyday life.

The opposite direction of meaning production in affective semiosis is bottom-up. The encounter unfolds from level 0 and first the object becomes of interest because of some "qualities of feelings", then because it demands some "reaction against it", and then it becomes a "generalizing or associating element" (Peirce, 1958, 8.144) through the interpretant. For instance, I am walking in the countryside and happen to climb a small hill (Figure 6.12). From the top, I observe the landscape and I feel that the place has some special qualities (feeling); some emotional state emerges that demands some kind of interpretation by me (reaction to the feeling) (Level 1). The hill must have some supernatural qualities, maybe it is a "holy place" (association and generalization through interpretant, Level 2).

Once the sign complex has been produced, the hill becomes a sign of holiness (hyper-generalized level 4), and in the future I will probably visit the hill every time I want to have a spiritual experience. The bottom-up meaning-making according to the affective logic reads, "I feel something special in this place *therefore* it must be holy".

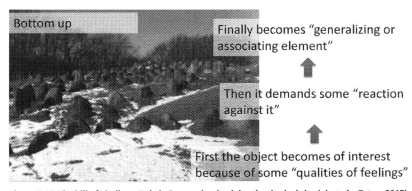

Figure 6.12 The hill of Lindhom Høje in Denmark, a burial archeological site (photo by Tateo, 2017)

The top-down and the bottom-up paths are different ways in which the person affectively relates to the environment through the mediation of the signs that are disseminated in the surroundings. They are not mutually exclusive and both are available when the person needs to make sense of a life experience. The affective logic is useful to understand the collectively coordinated human activities – for instance religion, art, war, education, leisure – in which a society needs to direct and control personal affective experiences and conduct.

SUMMARY OF CHAPTER 6

In Chapter 6, we have described the way cultural psychology conceives the human relating with the environment, both affectively and existentially. We have defined some features of person–world relations mediated by signs and characterized by:

- dilemmatic situations characterized by fuzziness, contemporary presence of cognitive, affective, ethical dimensions, mutually defining alternative courses of action. The meaning of the dilemma does not disappear once a choice is made.
- ambivalence, an inherent feature of semiosis and to a certain degree is functional to the meaning-making. Total absence or total ambivalence inhibit the functioning of semiosis.
- tensegrity, the structural tension produced through a constant labor required by the maintenance of the continuity/discontinuity dynamic of the self.
- affective logic, which describes how the person affectively relates to the world and how meaning emerges through different levels of signs generalization.

Check your knowledge and reflect

Task: Think about a significant experience in your life (e.g., first day of school; a significant event you have witnessed; a loss; etc.) and try to analyze your own experience using the concepts that you learned in this chapter. Write a short essay (maximum two pages; you can include images that you take) elaborating your personal reflections. Then, share your essay with two colleagues and ask for their feedback.

REFERENCES

Abbey, E. (2004). Circumventing ambivalence in identity: The importance of latent and overt aspects of symbolic meaning. *Culture & Psychology, 10*(3), 331–336.

Abbey, E., & Valsiner, J. (2005). Emergence of meanings through ambivalence. *Forum Qualitative Sozialforschung Forum: Qualitative Social Research*, 6(1). https://doi.org/10.17169/fqs-6.1.515

Ainsworth, M. D., Blehar, M. C., Waters, E., & Wall, S. (1978). *Patterns of attachment: A psychological study of the strange situation*. Hillsdale, NJ: Erlbaum.

Albarracin, J., Zanna, D., & Blair, M. (2005). *The handbook of attitudes*. Mahwah, NJ: Lawrence Erlbaum.

Bateson, G. (1972). *Steps to an ecology of mind: Collected essays in anthropology, psychiatry, evolution, and epistemology*. Chicago, IL: University Of Chicago Press.

Bateson, G., Jackson, D. D., Haley, J., & Weakland, J. (1956). Toward a theory of schizophrenia. *Behavioral Science*, 1, 251–264.

Blackman, L., & Venn, C. (2010). Affect. *Body & Society*, 16(1), 7–28.

Bleuler, P. E. (1911/1950). *Dementia praecox or the group of schizophrenias* (J. Zimkin, Trans.). New York: International Universities Press.

Cabell, K. R., & Valsiner, J. (Eds.). (2013). *The catalyzing mind: Beyond models of causality* (Vol. 11). New York: Springer Science & Business Media.

Chaudhary, N., Misra, G., Bansal, P., Valsiner, J., & Singh, T. (2022). Making sense of culture for the psychological sciences. *Review of General Psychology*, 26(4), 399–415.

DeMarree, K. G., Wheeler, S. C., Briñol, P., & Petty, R. E. (2014). Wanting other attitudes: Actual–desired attitude discrepancies predict feelings of ambivalence and ambivalence consequences. *Journal of Experimental Social Psychology*, 53, 5–18.

de Sousa Bastos, A. C. (2017). Shadow trajectories: The poetic motion of motherhood meanings through the lens of lived temporality. *Culture & Psychology*, 23(3), 408–422.

DeYoung, C. G., & Krueger, R. F. (2018). Understanding psychopathology: Cybernetics and psychology on the boundary between order and chaos. *Psychological Inquiry*, 29(3), 165–174.

Evans, J. S. B. (2020). Bounded rationality, reasoning and dual processing. In R. Viale (Ed.), *Routledge handbook of bounded rationality* (pp. 185–195). London: Routledge.

Freud, S. (1926). Inhibitions, symptoms and anxiety. *The standard edition of the complete psychological works of Sigmund Freud*, 20, 75–126. London: Macmillan.

Freud, S. (1955). Totem and taboo: Some points of agreement between the mental lives of savages and neurotics (1913 [1912–13]). In *The standard edition of the complete psychological works of Sigmund Freud*, 13, VII–162. London: Macmillan.

Fuller, R. B. (1961). Tensegrity. *Portfolio and Art News Annual*, 4, pp. 112–127.

Gigerenzer, G. (2020). What is bounded rationality? In R. Viale (Ed.), *Routledge handbook of bounded rationality* (pp. 55–69). London: Routledge.

Graubert, D. N., & Miller, J. S. A. (1957). On ambivalence. *The Psychiatric Quarterly*, 31(1–4), 458–464.

Gross, J. J. (1998). The emerging field of emotion regulation: An integrative review. *Review of General Psychology*, 2(3), 271.

Harrist, S. (2006). A phenomenological investigation of the experience of ambivalence. *Journal of Phenomenological Psychology*, 37(1), 85–114. https://doi.org/10.1163/156916206778150411

Hill, D. (2015). *Affect regulation theory: A clinical model*. New York: W.W. Norton.

Ingber, D. E. (2003). Tensegrity I. Cell structure and hierarchical systems biology. *Journal of Cell Science*, 116, 1157–1173.

Judge, A. (1978). Transcending duality through tensional integrity: Part I: A lesson in organization from building design, and Part 2: From systems-versus-networks to tensegrity organizations. *Transnational Association 5v*, pp. 248–57, 258–65.

Kaplan, K. J. (1972). On the ambivalence–indifference problem in attitude theory and measurement: A suggested modification of the semantic differential technique. *Psychological Bulletin*, 77, 361–372.

Kohlberg, L. (1981). *Essays on moral development, Vol l. I: The philosophy of moral development*. San Francisco, CA: Harper & Row.

Lennon, K. (2010). Re-enchanting the world: the role of imagination in perception. *Philosophy*, *85*(3), 375–389.

Lewin, K. (1936). *Principles of topological psychology*. New York and London: McGraw-Hill.

Lewin, K. (1939). Field theory and experiment in social psychology: Concepts and methods. *The American Journal of Sociology*, *44*(6), 868–896.

Maran, T. (2020). *Ecosemiotics: The study of signs in changing ecologies*. Cambridge, UK: Cambridge University Press.

Nichols, J. H. (1998). *Plato's Phaedrus*. Ithaca, NY & London: Cornell University Press.

Peirce, C. S. (1931–1958). *Collected papers of Charles Sanders Peirce*. Cambridge, MA: Harvard University Press.

Sawada, D., & Caley, M. T. (1985). Dissipative structures: New metaphors for becoming in education. *Educational Researcher*, *14*(3), 13–19.

Shweder, R. A., & Much, N. C. (1987). Determinations of meaning: Discourse and moral socialization. In W. M. Kurtines & J. L. Gewirtz (Eds.), *Moral development through social interaction* (pp. 197–244). New York: John Wiley & Sons.

Silva Filho, W. J., Dazzani, M. V. M., Tateo, L., Gottschalk Sukerman Barreto, R., & Marsico, G. (2023). He knows, she doesn't? Epistemic inequality in a developmental perspective. *Review of General Psychology*, *27*(3), 231–244.

Simmel, G. (1918/2010). *The view of life*. Four metaphysical essays with journal aphorisms, translated by J. A. Y. Andrews and D. N. Levine. Chicago, IL: University of Chicago Press.

Simmel, G. (1994). Bridge and door. *Theory, Culture & Society*, *11*(5), 5–10.

Smelser, N. J. (1998). The rational and the ambivalent in the social sciences: 1997 presidential address. *American Sociological Review*, *63*(1), 1–15.

Sturgeon, S. (2020). *The rational mind*. Oxford: Oxford University Press.

Swindell, J. S. (2010). Ambivalence. *Philosophical Explorations: An International Journal for the Philosophy of Mind and Action*, *13*(1), 23–34.

Tateo, L. (2018a). Ideology of success and the dilemma of education today. In A. Joerchel & G. Benetka (Eds.), *Memories of Gustav Ichheiser: Theory and history in the human and social sciences*. Springer, Cham. https://doi.org/10.1007/978-3-319-72508-6_9

Tateo, L. (2018b). Affective semiosis and affective logic. *New Ideas in Psychology*, *48*, 1–11.

Tateo, L. (2019). The journey of learning. *Mind, Culture, and Activity*, *26*(4), 371–382.

Tateo, L., & Marsico, G. (2013). The Self as tension of wholeness and emptiness. *Interacções*, 24, 1–19.

Valsiner, J. (2020). *Sensuality in human living: The cultural psychology of affect*. Cham: Springer.

Valsiner, J. (2021). *General human psychology*. New York: Springer.

Valsiner, J., & Rudolph, L. (2017). Who shall survive? Psychology that replaces quantification with qualitative mathematics. In E. Abbey & S. Sugarn (Eds.), *Emerging methods in psychology* (pp. 121–140). New York: Routledge.

Williams, S. (2001). *Emotions and social theory*. London: Sage.

Yahya, A. H., & Sukmayadi, V. (2020). A review of cognitive dissonance theory and its relevance to current social issues. *MIMBAR: Jurnal Sosial Dan Pembangunan*, *36*(2), 480–488.

Zeigarnik, B. (1967). On finished and unfinished tasks. In W. D. Ellis (Ed.), *A sourcebook of Gestalt psychology*. New York: Humanities Press.

Index

Abduction, 82, 95, 103, 106
activity, 9, 27–29, 31, 70–72, 75, 96, 101, 141
adaptation, 16, 25, 70, 77, 143
affectivating, 2, 69, 148
affective logic, 4, 128, 147, 150–152
agency, 50, 67, 70, 72, 129, 133
agent, 23, 45, 53, 65, 73, 80, 116, 122, 129, 137, 140
ambivalence, 4, 17, 79, 121, 129, 131, 134–142, 145, 148–149
Aristotle, 10, 66
artifact, 3, 5, 21, 28–31, 43, 53, 63, 67, 73, 89, 98, 113, 116, 121, 150
axiom, 11, 12, 17, 26, 31, 39, 42, 70, 79, 90

Bakhtin, M., 39, 45, 71
Baldwin, J. M., 25, 26, 101
Bateson, G., 137
behavior, 10, 25, 29, 32, 38, 50, 51, 65–67, 70, 75, 113, 118, 120, 130, 136, 142, 145
belief, 27, 29, 50, 80, 89, 91, 92, 100, 103, 129
binary, 10, 14, 79, 81, 131,
Bleuler, P. E., 134–135
Boas, F. U., 64
border, 11, 14, 18, 63, 75, 98, 100, 110–118, 133, 139, 143, 144, 148
   border crossing, 116
   boundary, 11, 31, 114, 138
   general genetic law of bordering development, 121, 122

bordering, 110, 115, 121, 123, 128, 148
Bruner, J. S., 27, 48, 50–52, 70
buffer, 14, 143, 145

canonicity, 50, 52
causality, 131
child, 25–27, 30, 68, 73, 75, 100, 101–103, 117, 123
chronotope, 39
cogenetic logic, 10, 13, 15, 73
cognition, 69, 72
cognitive closure, 17
Cole, M., 28–30, 69, 78
collectively coordinated, 26, 69, 72, 152,
commodity, 24, 102,
complementarity, 94–96, 99, 104, 116, 146
condition, 14–18, 20, 22, 30, 39, 48, 62, 65, 76, 90, 94–96, 104, 112, 115, 117, 130, 135, 137, 142, 143, 145
context, 22, 28–30, 32, 41, 42–45, 49, 50, 65, 69, 70, 73, 75, 77, 78, 80, 94, 101, 116, 133, 142, 146
continuity, 4, 60, 103, 121
critical, 54, 72, 81, 128
cross-cultural psychology, 78
cultivation, 30, 60, 63, 69
cultural-historical, 26, 28, 44, 69, 71
culture, 10, 23, 30, 45, 49, 63–69, 76, 104, 122, 135, 146
   collective and personal, 72, 75, 148
Customizability, 51

155

decolonization, 78–81
development, 14, 21, 26, 27, 30, 42, 46, 50, 54, 73, 75, 100, 101, 116–118, 123
  cultural development, 31, 64, 70
  moral development, 133
Diachronicity, 50
Dialogical Self Theory, 46
dialogicality, 44–45, 52, 75
dialogue, 45–46, 50, 70, 75, 82, 114, 121, 138, 141
dilemma, 130–131, 133, 137
dilemmatic field, 132, 134, 142
discontinuity, 67, 121, 130
distinction, 10–12, 14–15, 22, 63, 67, 113–116, 119, 121
Dragestil, 61
Driesch, H. A. E., 39, 40
dyadic, 21, 32
dynamic system, 113
dynamic totality, 127

ecosystem, 51, 78–82
educated intuition, 54
education, 100, 104, 123, 137
emotion, 31, 47, 69, 71, 129, 134, 143, 146, 147–149, 151
environment, 16, 26, 30–32, 41, 45, 63, 67–68, 70, 73, 76, 98–100, 110, 116, 119, 122, 138, 142–145, 148, 150
epistemology, 45, 53, 71, 81,
externalization, 30, 32, 119, 122, 150,

Freud, S., 42, 100, 135
future, 16, 19, 22, 40–44, 52, 62, 92–94, 103, 118, 146, 151

Ganzheitspsychologie, 71
Gegenstand, 73, 114, 116–118, 121, 131–133,
generalization, 79, 82, 93, 149, 151,
genetic, 31, 43, 70, 121

Herbst, P. G., 10–12
Hermans, H., 46
history of psychology, 5, 42
Homogeneity, 65
human activity, 28, 105,
human experience, 15, 42, 69, 73, 93, 100

Imagination, 73, 93–94, 101, 104
  Scientific imagination, 95

Expansive and reductive imagination, 97
Imaginative process, 29, 62, 90, 94, 96, 99, 100–102, 104, 138
inclusive separation, 13, 114
inhibition, 98, 118
injustice, 6, 55
Intentionality, 50, 133
interaction, 24, 28, 31–32, 43, 45, 48, 68, 72, 92, 96, 100, 102, 121, 138, 145
internalization, 25, 30, 32, 73, 98, 101, 119, 123,
Interpretant, 21–23, 115, 119, 122, 134, 151
I-position, 46
irreversible time, 39–42, 50, 55, 91, 145, 150

James, W., 113
Jung, C. G., 97,
Justifying, 50

Kohlberg, L., 132–134
Kull, K., 67–68

Lazarus, M., 70–71
learning, 23, 25, 75, 123,
Lewin, K., 31, 143
Luria, A., 26–27

Marková, I., 45, 48
Marsico, G., 113, 119
Marx, K., 26
meaning-making, 16–19, 24, 31, 38–39, 45, 52, 55, 69, 90, 99, 116, 119, 121, 139, 146, 148, 151
mediation, 21, 25–32, 71, 76, 90, 93, 98,
Meinong, A., 114
memento mori, 98
mental experiment, 94, 131, 134
mental function, 45, 71, 98, 104, 116,
  higher-level, 66, 69, 93, 98–100, 103
  lower level, 66
meta-code, 53, 129
methodological cycle, 53–55, 128
methodology, 43, 46, 53
migration, 77, 102
mind-wandering, 94
Modal thinking, 50
motivation, 104, 117

narrative thought, 48
narrativity, 46, 49–52

negation, 10, 12, 14, 115
normative, 13, 137, 142

ontogenesis, 103, 116
opposite, 53, 63, 98, 114, 129, 134, 137, 146, 151
orientation, 42, 47, 92, 116–118, 122

paradigmatic thought, 48
Peirce, C. S., 20–22, 132
perception, 29, 72, 98, 101, 148,
Perspective taking, 49
Phaedrus, 129, 141
phenomenology, 72, 110
Piaget, J., 42, 101
Plato, 129
polyphony, 46, 52
polysemy, 120
Positioning, 49, 52
primary operation, 10, 113
proculturation, 60, 77
promotion, 118
psychological field, 143

qualities, 4, 24, 29, 44, 53, 72, 112, 151,

rationality, 96, 129–130, 148
reflection, 69, 103
Representamen, 21–23, 150
resistance, 81, 116–118, 132, 143

sarcophagus model, 65–66
self, 45–46, 76, 121, 145
semiosis, 20–21, 27, 39, 41, 55, 115, 138,
sign, 20–24, 26–27, 41, 46, 52, 63, 71, 73, 76, 99, 119, 137, 141, 150
   border-sign 115, 119, 123
   field-like sign, 147
   function of sign 29
   hierarchy of signs 149
   system of signs 67, 139
   types of sign, 23, 113, 138

Simmel, G., 113, 121, 147
substitution, 22, 115, 120
symbolic, 14, 24, 27, 50, 68, 71, 101, 121, 138
   symbolic resource 78, 146
systemic organization, 69, 105, 121

teaching, 54,69,
temporality, 22, 39, 43, 50, 54, 93, 115, 120
tensegrity, 142, 144–146
tension, 14, 17, 44, 50, 81, 88, 123, 129, 133, 142, 144–146
third-level psychological processes, 2, 69
tool, 24, 26–28, 31, 75, 78, 92, 94, 98, 101, 123
triadic set, 11–12

Umgebung, 98, 100
Umwelt, 45,67, 91, 98–99, 103
uncertainty, 17, 21, 98, 116, 129, 138, 141, 146
uncoupling, 93–94
unification, 22, 26, 115, 120
unit of analysis, 71

Valsiner, J., 3, 13, 32, 41, 45, 54, 73, 75, 114, 116, 149
values, 46,77, 80, 115, 132, 150
Vico, G., 70
Vygotsky, L. S., 24, 31, 45, 71, 92, 96, 101, 104, 117–118,
Völkerpsychologie, 70–71

Wertsch, J., 28, 69
window of acceptable possibilities, 73–74, 76–77, 142, 148, 150
Wundt, W., 71

Zeigarnik's effect, 143
Zittoun, T., 26, 78, 93, 145
Zone of Potential Estrangement, 80–82
Zone of proximal development, 118

Printed in the United States
by Baker & Taylor Publisher Services